YOUR STORY SELLS

HOW TO LEVERAGE TRANSPARENCY, AUTHENTICITY, AND GROWTH TO SUCCEED IN BUSINESS

Your Story Sells

Copyright © 2023

All rights reserved. No part of this publication may be reproduced or transmitted in any form or by any means including photocopy, recording, or through other electronic or mechanical methods, without written permission from the author and contributors, except in cases of brief quotations embodied in critical reviews and certain noncommercial uses permitted by copyright law.

The author, publisher, and contributors shall not be liable for any misuse of the enclosed material. This book is strictly for informational and educational purposes only. The author, publisher, and contributors do not guarantee that anyone following these techniques, suggestions, tips, ideas, or strategies will heal or become successful. The author, publisher, and contributors shall have neither liability nor responsibility to anyone with respect to any loss or damage caused, or alleged to be caused, directly or indirectly, by the information or suggestions contained in this book.

To the extent that any business, investment, or financial strategies are shared, they are shared for informational and educational purposes only. This book does not guarantee results or provide legal, tax, investment, or financial advice. Consult your legal, tax, investment, or financial professional.

To the extent that any medical or health information is shared in this book, it is shared as an information and education resource only and is not to be used or relied on for any diagnostic or treatment purposes. Any such information is not intended to be patient information, does not create any patient-physician relationship, and should not be used as a substitute for professional diagnosis and treatment. Neither the author, publisher, nor contributors provide health or healing advice. Consult your healthcare professional.

Published by Made to Change the World™ Publishing
Nashville, Tennessee

Cover and interior design by Chelsea Jewell and Lynnea Teters

ISBN: 978-1-956837-15-5 Hardcover
ISBN: 978-1-956837-16-2 eBook

Printed in the USA, Canada, Australia, and Europe

This book is dedicated to you—to the greatness in you, to the dream that you showed up on the planet to make reality, and to the story that you're about to tell.

Know that you are enough, you are worthy, you have what it takes, and the world is waiting on your gift.

Shine your light. Use your voice. Tell your story.

Yours in greatness,
Les Brown—Mamie's Baby Boy

CONTENTS

FOREWORD
Maya Comerota — vii

INTRODUCTION
Ellie D. Shefi — xvii

YOUR STORY SELLS: HOW TO LEVERAGE TRANSPARENCY, ACCEPTANCE, AND GROWTH TO SUCCEED IN BUSINESS
Les Brown — 01

WEALTH GROWS ON TREES
Jerremy Alexander Newsome — 13

INSPIRED IMPACT
Kate Butler — 29

WHO CAN I CONNECT YOU WITH?
Winnona Gaviglio — 45

MY IDENTITY, MY DESTINY
David Grace — 59

THE PAIN WAS THE PATH ALL ALONG
Nafsheen Luhar — 77

MY WISHES FOR YOU
Raul Lopez Jr. — 99

THE BEST LAID PLANS
Jenny Infante-Reyes — 113

YOUR STORY IS YOUR SUPERPOWER
Ellie D. Shefi 131

A NOTE FROM ME TO YOU
Les Brown 145

YOUR MESSAGE MATTERS, YOUR STORY SELLS!
Made to Change the World™ Publishing Team 146

AUTHOR PERMISSIONS 147

FOREWORD
Maya Comerota

You're here for a reason. There's someone you were born to be. You want to make an impact and share your most authentic self with the world. You want to laugh, play, and have fun. You want more passion, creativity, and aliveness.

You know that there is something that you were born for, something you came into this life to do. There is something that is uniquely yours that no one else can do.

Your uniqueness is your power, and there's a dream, a life, that is yearning to express through you. It's time to step into the full embodiment of you, live your dream, and *be who you were born to be*!

Part of leaning into the truth of who you are is discovering and sharing your story. It is through your story that you build the brand, business, impact, and life you desire.

Throughout the pages of *Your Story Sells*, Les Brown, Ellie Shefi, Kate Butler, and other luminaries will guide you toward creating impact in the world through the power of your message and your story. Your story is the portal to living the life you want to live … to becoming the person you were born to be!

But just how do you uncover your story, you wonder?

It took me many years to reveal, acknowledge, embrace, and share the story of who I truly am—without the titles, without the roles, just me. But since I have, my life has so much more meaning, is joyous, adventurous, and abundant—full of living, laughing, and loving! And now it's my life's mission to help others discover and tap into who they are born to be. As crazy as it sounded at first, I realized I was born to guide others to see that they too are magnificent by design, they too are born for something, and they too can live a legendary life.

The Chrysalis

Each one of us has a unique mission to fulfill on this Earth in this lifetime that is beautiful in its own right as it contributes to the whole of the universe.

I had risen up the corporate ladder and had an incredible career. I had a husband, a son, and everything one could possibly want. From the outside looking in, anyone would think, "Maya has it all." And yet, there was a part of me that was yearning for more. I didn't know what that "more" was. And I felt guilty for wanting it. It's so common to feel like you shouldn't want more. After all, what more could there be when you have a family, a career, and all those things? What more is there?

I found out one summer Sunday afternoon.

I was in my office working—because I would often work on Sundays—while my three-year-old son would play downstairs. I could hear him laughing and giggling with the nanny. All of me wanted to go downstairs and play with him, but there was a part of me that felt so stuck to the computer, doing what I was doing. I honestly didn't know if he would even choose me anymore because I hadn't been playful with him in so long.

As I was working away, I got a ding on my computer, and I realized, "I can't do this anymore." I grabbed the car keys, ran downstairs, and told my son, "Hunter, mommy will be right back." He said, "Mommy, take me with you." I said, "No, little guy, I'll be back very soon." I jumped into the car and drove away. Twenty minutes later, I was in front of a red light and couldn't remember how I got there. As I turned the wheel to approach the on-ramp, a huge black SUV crashed into the side of my car. Everything started spinning. Everything was in slow motion. The SUV flew through the railing, through the green sign, and down the embankment. It stopped a second before reaching oncoming traffic.

As I watched the SUV fly through the air, I thought, "Please don't let that person die. Don't let there be a child in that car." My car was spinning, and I was buckling in my womb. I noticed the car seat that was right behind me. My son was nearly in it. As everything was spinning, I saw visions of what I believed was my funeral. I didn't know if I was going to come out alive. I felt a voice in every part of my body, and it said, "You didn't do what you came here to do."

I felt so much sadness and regret that I hadn't yet done what I came here to do. I had already done a lot in my life. I had run corporate teams, and I had a leadership team of three hundred people. That was probably the first moment that I prayed to God. I said, "If I make it out of here alive, I'll be her. I will be the woman I'm born to be. I don't know who that is. I don't know who I am without the titles and roles of mother, sister, wife, but I will be her if I make it out alive."

Twenty minutes later, the police arrived. The other woman and I were embracing. They looked at us and said, "How did you get out of there?" Both cars were completely totaled. I knew there was only one reason we survived that day and neither one of us had a scratch on us. That was the start of recognizing that there's something more that I'm here for. At the time, I didn't know what that was, but I was determined to go on a journey and figure out what I was born to do.

Born For This

What would you love?

Identifying what you're here for can be a very disorienting journey, especially at first: "How do I figure out who I was born to be? What feelings are authentic; which ones do I lean into? Where do I even start?"

I didn't know at the time, but step one is always, "What would you love?" I knew what I didn't love and would've said: "I don't want to work so hard. I don't want to work eighty hours a week. I don't want to be away from my child. I don't want to leave him in the morning before he wakes up and come home after he has gone to bed. I don't want to be like ships passing in the night with my husband where we barely spend any time together." I knew I didn't want any of that. But what did I want?

I thought, "I would love to have dates with my husband, feel inspired and alive, and go on adventures. I would love to be an amazing leader that supports a balance between home and work and be an inspiration where people can live their best life and do their best work without compromising or sacrificing themselves." *What would you love*—that was the key question. Because I didn't know that question back then, I navigated clumsily, following instinct: "This feeling. Oh, I like this feeling! That's it. I'll follow that."

I just knew I needed to be alive, and I had this second chance. I saw my life pass me by, and I felt regret. Nobody ever wants to feel that level of regret—that if your life is over, you haven't yet lived and done what you came here to do, or shared with the people that you loved. I knew I had to figure this out.

I started to notice curiosity, passions, and fire deep inside, and it brought me alive. So every time I felt that little flame, fire, spark, inspiration, and curiosity inside of me, I followed it. It wasn't often that I felt it because I was numb to many things. So when I felt it, I knew it with certainty. It was like, "I love this. I'm passionate about this. I'm curious about this." I would lean into that. Now I call it your life force, but back then I recognized it as curiosity, inspiration, and passion. That's where it started, by following that passion, inspiration, or little flame. Each little spark was guiding me toward my personal responses to "What would you love?"

Today when I work with clients, I always begin there. It's such a seemingly simple question, but it truly helps you figure out what you were born to be and to do. As you answer, you'll reveal the path that leads to the legacy you want to live and leave. Asking that question is something that you can do regardless of where you are in your life. If you don't love what's going on or if you don't love your life, what would you love? It's such a powerful question that will guide you to celebrate and say:

I was born for this!

Your X Factor

You are born for something, and you are given experiences in your life to support you to do that very thing.

As you become more aware of and get more comfortable with embracing what you love and leaning into what you were born to do, you'll become ready to unleash your X factor—that unique combination of knowledge, skills, and passions that make up *you*. It's what generates that inner fire that will propel you and drive you forward in business, relationships, and life.

I believe that we are born for something. We are given experiences in our life to support us to do that very thing. All the stories in my life, all the trials, tribulations, and triumphs were all gifted to me so that I can share and be who I am uniquely in the world. No one has had the same exact human experience as I have had. No one has my story. Just like no one has your story. It's up to you to discover it, and it's up to you to share it.

You have a unique life curriculum, and you can use that to identify your X factor and craft your story. Tap into your life experience and how that has made you an expert. You're an expert at you, just as I'm an expert at me! Your life experience is the reason your message and your mission resonates with you and those you'd like to serve, just as my life experience resonates with me and the millions of people I serve globally.

Oftentimes, our X factor and passions are born out of things that we weren't able to express at some point. So tapping into it helps us reconnect to our life force, message, and mission. If you're hearing a voice say, "You're not doing what you're here to do. There's something more!" pay attention to the voice! It's your life force—your energy—and it is consistently communicating with you. It's imploring you to commit: "I've got to do that thing. I was created for that thing. I don't want to get to the end and realize I didn't do the thing or become the person that I was supposed to become." If you're hearing your life force calling to you, and you're responding, "There is something that I'm born for. There's a thing that I'm meant to share with the world. There's an impact that I meant to make. Maybe I'm not making that impact yet, but it's burning inside of me, and I want to express it to the world," then you're ready to identify and dive into your X factor.

These deep explorations can be challenging. I work with clients to identify their X factor and then to cultivate it. I guide them to start with the end in mind. Imagine you're at the end of your life. You have hours or a day to live. Who would you want to be? What would you want to say? What would you want to share? We all have something inside of us that, if our life ended tomorrow, we would want to make sure we did or said. I support my clients with a totally immersive and transformational process to tap into that unique something that they are born for, that life that is yearning to express through them so they experience more passion, freedom, prosperity, creativity, and love.

Be YOU Now

Before anybody else can believe in you, you must believe in you.
Before anyone else will choose you, you must choose you.

Once you've started to embrace your X factor, it's time to show up in the world in the authenticity and alignment of being you. Time to come home to yourself and become the person that you were divinely made to be. Allow yourself to be who you are created to be. There's a reason why you are here; it's not by accident.

Are you ready to step into, embody, and fully be who you were born to be right now? To be YOU now means to hold that dream, that image that's given to you, to see it and feel it, and to lean into it every day.

I hold an image of me as a world-class transformational teacher who, by my beingness, can transform lives. It's not because of what I say or do but because of *who I am*. I believe we all have that capability. I invite my clients to create a very powerful image of who they are, what they believe in, and what they stand for. And then ask themselves: "If this image is true, then who am I at this moment? What do I choose at this moment? Who am I as a spouse? Who am I as a parent? Who am I as a friend? Who am I as a colleague? Who am I as a client?" Through this process, my clients get to choose to be themselves now every day. Every day won't be perfect, but the fire is built by creating this image and persona of the person that they know they can be.

You too can recognize and realize that there is someone you're here to be. Just being that person is what will lead you to be happy, fulfilled, confident, authentic, prosperous, and passionate. Be one hundred percent you. Tap into your X factor, that thing that you uniquely are here to be and do, and then share that with others. When you do, you'll have uncommon success. It's because you're you, and the world needs you.

It's now time to write your story, the story only you can share. So tap into your X factor, and show up in the world fully as you. When you show up authentically as you, *that's* the story that sells! Now go out and tell your story.

You are born for this!

—Maya

ABOUT MAYA COMEROTA

Maya is a transformational teacher and coach, intuitive guide, speaker, and #1 international best-selling author. Through her signature programs, Born For This, Living Legendary, Living Luminary, and X Factor, she has supported over two million people worldwide to discover their unique gifts and ignite the fire of their dreams so they can live a life they absolutely love.

Maya has a unique gift of guiding people back home to their heart and spirit so they can live the life they were born to live.

She has been a featured expert speaker with Tony Robbins, Dean Graziosi, and Mary Morrisey, amongst many others, and she has been featured on media outlets such as NBC, ABC, CBS, FOX, *Entrepreneur*, and *Rolling Stone Magazine*.

You may have recently seen Maya at the Time to Thrive Challenge with Tony Robbins and Dean Graziosi, and she is now also the managing director of Legacy Mastermind with Dean Graziosi and Brendon Burchard.

Connect with Maya and transform your world at mayacomerota.com.

INTRODUCTION
Ellie D. Shefi

Have you ever wondered why some people, like Les Brown, Maya Comerota, and the other experts in this book, effortlessly attract a loyal following and build successful businesses while others struggle to gain traction? The secret lies in the power of personal storytelling.

In today's world, where everyone is vying for attention, it's not enough to simply have a great product or service. You need to have an authentic, aligned brand that fosters a connection with your audience, builds trust, and differentiates you from the competition. And what better way to do that than by sharing your story in books, on stage, and in the media?

Your story is unique. It's what makes your business stand out. It's what makes your brand yours. Yes, YOU are your brand. By sharing your struggles, successes, and lessons learned, you can establish the know, like, and trust factor with your audience, inspire them to take action, and increase your impact and income.

Your Story, Your Message

You're an expert in your field who is excited to share your knowledge, services, and products with the world. You KNOW that there are people waiting for what you have to offer. But they don't yet know you. They don't know the blood, sweat, and tears that you've spent gaining your expertise. The challenges that you've overcome. The absolute delight that you feel when you share your products and services—yourself, really—with them. They don't yet know your story, your message!

You're reading this book because you have a message that you want to share with the world! And your message is important! It's the packaged result of all that makes you YOU—it's your unique combination of everything you've experienced and learned throughout your life. Lessons learned from traditional education and lessons learned through failing and falling and getting knocked down but getting up again! It's these hard-learned and hard-earned lessons that are exactly why your message will establish your credibility and authority and position you as the go-to expert in your field.

And you share your message to the world through *your story*. Your story is your superpower. Afterall, only you can create it! Your story is what positions you uniquely in the world. And it's the vehicle that reaches your right-fit clients and delivers *your unique impact*. No longer will your hard-earned skills remain unseen, unheard, and undiscovered. Your story is the genesis of becoming a globally-recognized brand. You want to tell it with transparency and authenticity. Afterall, your story is the gateway to the life, business, and impact that you desire. It's time to stop being the best-kept secret! Yes, it's time for the world to know who you are!

Like the experts in this book, you too can craft and hone an authentic, aligned story that will convert with your ideal clients. You too can monetize your expertise through sharing your story powerfully in books, on stages, and in the media. You too can use your story to systematically and predictably grow your audience and scale your income to seven figures and beyond.

Share Your Story

Once you're clear on the message you want to convey—the story you want to share—how do you get it into the world? How do you turn your expertise into an income stream and position yourself as the undeniable expert in your field? How do you identify your dream client, the person who needs to hear your message? And how do you attract that dream client and connect with them?

Write Your Story

The best vehicle to get your message out there, to connect with ideal clients, to create impact, and to build a global brand around your story is to become a best-selling author. That's right! Writing a best-selling book serves two very important purposes.

First, as a bestseller, it will position you as the preeminent expert in your field. Becoming a best-selling author is the key to building the brand and business you desire, to creating more impact and more income. It opens the door for media exposure, speaking opportunities, and increased visibility. How do you ensure that your book is a bestseller? Partner with a proven publisher that has years of experience in helping writers strategically craft a manuscript that converts; has world-class, detail-oriented professional editing and designing services that ensure your finished book clearly represents your business and your brand, positions you as the undeniable expert you are, and is impressive to read; and develops a detailed launch strategy designed to ensure your book gets in front of the right audiences and becomes a bestseller.

Second, whether you're sharing your story or sharing your knowledge, processes, or tips, someone is waiting for you to get your book out of your head and into the world. If there's one thing I've learned from having over thirty years of experience writing, editing, ghostwriting, and *publishing thousands of pieces*, it's this: Writing your story will transform *you*; but sharing it will transform the *world*!

So what are you waiting for? It's time to share your story, become a best-selling author, and leverage your best-selling book!

Create Content from Your Story

Beyond gaining the accolade of being a best-selling author and the credibility boost that comes from it, writing your book also gives you a ready-made content machine! Yes, you can repurpose the content of your book as your marketing content. Need to produce a newsletter? A blog? Emails? Social media content? No problem! It's right there in your book, just waiting for you! Use it to build your following, build rapport with your target audience, and build your authentic, aligned brand.

Speak Your Story

Once your story is being shared via your best-selling book and emails, newsletters, blogs, and social media content derived from your ready-made supply of easily-accessible content, it's time to amplify your message and your presence. It's time for you to increase your authority, visibility, and income. Yes, it's time to share your story from the stage.

So, how do you do that? First, create a story bank filled with the stories you tell to demonstrate key points your ideal clients need to know. Then, craft your signature talk utilizing stories from your story bank that will capture the attention of your ideal clients. You must create a captivating message and convert your audience with confidence. You'll have to develop the key components of your message that will drive conversions AND learn how to effortlessly customize that message based on the type of appearance, audience, and goal. Being able to powerfully and confidently connect and convert from stage is critical to building the brand and the business you desire, so of course, you must also practice techniques for building that confidence, connection, and trust with your audience so that you leverage your appearances and get the great results you desire.

After mastering the stage, it's time to dive into media appearances! Conduct outreach to find the best media hosts and producers while building out your connection strategy that captures the media's attention and differentiates you from your competition. Additionally, develop an irresistible media pitch to get podcast, radio, YouTube, TV, and event producers to say yes.

Mastering the media leads to amazing partnerships, opportunities, and high-quality leads that come from high-profile media exposure. It's how you supercharge your visibility and grow your brand!

Scale Your Story

So you're sharing your story in books, on stages, and in the media, and people are receiving it—now what?

It's time to drive people to you, to monetize your message. Here is where you develop irresistible offers and share your expertise through your programs, courses, and workshops, consulting and advising, coaching, leading retreats and masterminds—all services to bring people to you. And throughout your programs, you will continue to share your story, authentically and transparently. This is how you use your story to build a business, become the undisputed go-to expert in your field, and become a global brand. This is how your story sells! Go tell it!

I can't wait to hear your story!

—Ellie

ABOUT ELLIE D. SHEFI

Ellie Shefi is an attorney, advisor, leadership consultant, corporate trainer, keynote speaker, strategist, and #1 international best-selling and award-winning author who helps organizations optimize their culture and individuals expand their influence.

As the founder of MTC Consulting, Ellie leverages her more than thirty years of experience in law, business, education, and advocacy to help organizations build resilient teams and world-class cultures while developing influential leaders. Serving as a strategic advisor to governments, universities, corporations, entrepreneurs, and NGOs, she has successfully helped organizations mitigate their risk, optimize their operations, and align their teams.

Through her signature programs: Monetize Your Expertise™, Monetize Your Message™, and Master the Media™, Ellie helps entrepreneurs, leaders, coaches, and consultants become global brands by sharing their story in books, on stage, and in the media.

Dedicated to empowering others to use their voice, Ellie founded Made to Change the World™ Publishing, a full-service independent publishing house, where she guides aspiring best-selling authors through the writing and publishing process and helps leaders amplify their message so they can scale their impact.

A sought-after speaker, Ellie is regularly interviewed in top publications and on podcasts and media channels like *Forbes*, *Entrepreneur*, NBC, ABC, and CBS, amongst others, and she hosts the *Free by Design*™ television show, the *Creating an Impervious Mind*® YouTube series, and the *You Are Not Your Scars*® podcast.

Ellie is also the founder of the Made 2 Change the World™ Foundation, an emerging nonprofit organization that equips and empowers the next generation with the tools, resources, and strategies they need to create the lives, communities, and world they envision.

To connect with Ellie and learn more about her services, visit ellieshefi.com.

Marketing is no longer about the stuff that you make, but about the stories you tell.

— Seth Godin

YOUR STORY SELLS:
HOW TO LEVERAGE TRANSPARENCY, ACCEPTANCE, AND GROWTH TO SUCCEED IN BUSINESS

Les Brown

You are enough.
You have what it takes.
The world is waiting on your gift.

I heard these words before, but never did I think they applied to me. I was a poor, adopted boy who internalized the fact my birth mother did not want me and gave me up for adoption. I was grateful for my adopted mother, Mamie Brown, who had a loving heart but no money to raise us seven adopted children. But what she had was determination to give us the best possible life no matter the circumstances. To be honest, I was not an easy kid to discipline and rear. I was labeled Educable Mentally Retarded (EMR), had behavior problems, and was separated from most of my friends in school. Because of our economic situation, I wore second-hand clothes and had shoes that only fit my feet after stretching them in bathwater. By any standards, I was doomed.

Furthermore, I failed twice in school and was called "DT, the dumb twin." My twin brother was the good, smart, poised, standout student. I later learned that out of the 356 students in my graduating class, I was ranked 355—second to last—and was awarded my diploma based on attendance, or perhaps because I was too old to continue attending school, or the teachers were sick of me pulling fire alarms and pranks throughout the day. While I tried to do better, I was an embarrassment to myself and family members. I was the butt of jokes amongst friends, and, arguably, my future was limited.

In spite of my circumstances, there was one teacher who changed my life with nine words. Mr. Washington said, "Never let someone's opinion of you become your reality." It took some time to process; however, every time someone placed a limit on me or my abilities, those words, "Never let someone's opinion of you become your reality," bubbled up in me as a reminder that there was more to life. And I was determined to find it.

Every time I found myself up against the wall, I had to tell myself, "Les, it gets better." This did several things for me:

1. It gave me hope for the future. My present circumstances did not define me forever.

2. Knowing that it gets better provided me a sense of relief.

3. The pushback on my grim reality gave me breathing room and allowed me to practice optimism by helping me to strategically think my way out of challenging times.

In life's toughest moments, I found my strengths and talents; ironically, they were magnified. I mentioned that I was a handful and the butt of jokes. But I also had friends and family members engaged in me, my conversations, and jokes. I'm sure that they often wondered, "What is crazy Les going to do next?" But because they hung onto every word, joke, and insight I shared, I realized that I had a God-given personality, gifts, and talents. I just had to figure out how to make them work for my good.

I once heard a powerful quote: "Truth is within ourselves. We must open a way for the imprisoned splendor to escape." I discovered that the imprisoned splendor was myself, my personality, my natural talents, and, of course, my voice. In all of my career paths, I realized, I could not hide who I was to fit into someone else's box. When I was a sanitation worker, I was still the funny man. When I worked as a television salesman, my personality and passion were evident to my customers, and my sales commissions reflected my intensity. When I took a stab at becoming a local radio disc jockey, I did not shy away from being me. I laughed when things were funny, I continued to tell jokes, and I found that people loved me just being me. I was an open, transparent guy, who unapologetically discussed my failures and successes. While in my early years, I was a misfit to my family, I always concluded everything with, "This has been Mamie's Baby Boy." This closing statement was not a planned marketing ploy. It was me, that troubled little boy, Les Brown, paying homage to the woman who took me in as her son whom I was trying to make proud. Yet, audiences across the country loved my mentioning of my mother, and it stuck.

My Wit. My Voice. My Story. My Truth.

What is your truth, and how can it impact the lives of others? I've noticed that we all love a good story. We love good guys. We despise bad guys. We want a hero. We yearn to see the villain defeated. And we crave a happy ending. It was not my intention, but this is the formula that worked for my speaking career. Truthfully, my story is painful to recall and tell. For some, it is even painful to hear. Yet, it is the truth, and while I share my intimate space with others, I find that people become vulnerable and have a desire to share their story too, no matter how difficult it is. Truth is powerful and liberating; it can reshape lives.

To paraphrase Maya Angelou, "There is nothing more painful than an untold story buried in your soul." Stories are healing. Within them lie transformative powers waiting to be released into the hearts and minds of countless wounded souls in need of restoration. Wow! I love helping people, and if you are reading this book, you must share the same sentiments. What if telling your story helps you prevent someone from ending their life? What if sharing your lessons when you failed gives hope for someone else to keep on their journey? There is always someone who needs your voice, experience, and expertise. They can only hear it from you. Know that your voice is a projection of your vision, vibrancy, and power in the world. Each person has their own pitch, range, tone, and unique melody which characterize the sounds of their life. When you connect with your voice, you realize and own the responsibility for creating your greatest life.

Here are a few suggestions to help you move yourself, your story, and your business to the next level.

1. Align yourself with your purpose.

2. Follow your passion with a strong sense of optimism.

3. Remember, obstacles are opportunities.

It was L.C. Robinson who said, "Things may happen to you, and things may happen around you, but the only thing that ultimately matters, is what happens in you." You will discover so much growth internally as you overcome roadblocks, setbacks, and disappointments. But when you are aligned with your purpose, there is nothing that can derail you. In fact, you will be reintroduced to your unique greatness and gifts in profound ways while maximizing opportunities to make a substantial impact for generations to come. I remember even my mother saying to me, "I did not know how you were going to turn out boy. You were so much trouble." As I reflect, this makes me smile. But the truth is, I was always in touch with some aspect of my unique identity and passion because I always stood out, even if it was not in the best light.

I invite you to not be discouraged with children who seem to misbehave because they may only need one person to believe in them ... hear one encouraging word ... or receive one opportunity to change their lives. Likewise, I encourage you to not be so hard on yourself! If you have spent years off track, get back on track. Find a mentor, read books to enlighten you, and—here's my best tip—watch successful people, and do what they do. To be honest, you are one decision away from changing your life; which way you go is up to you. You will find that once you embark on a path to maximize personal talents or contributions through work or a cause, discovering your true purpose is inevitable.

YOUR

Y- You are the only one who can get out of your way to discover the real YOU.

O- Optimism. It is not enough to be skilled. It is not enough to be talented. It is essential that you believe in the possibilities for yourself and to expect good things to happen. Challenges will come; use that reservoir of positive expectation to stay strong and make you unstoppable.

U- Understand you cannot figure everything out, but do not lose hope.

R- Release the fear of an imagined problem keeping you from working on real solutions.

STORY

S- Story. I learned how one well-crafted and powerfully-delivered story not only can change others, but can be the source of healing and freedom to the storyteller.

T- Tough work. It is tough to be honest and transparent with your truth, especially if it is painful. Yet, it is even tougher to sit on your gifts and talents and watch others live their dreams.

O- Opportunity. You are always surrounded by opportunities and challenges. One of the big problems is being so focused on the challenge, or the threat of a challenge, that you let the opportunity pass right by—unnoticed and untapped.

R- Relationships. You do not reach the top of your potential by your own efforts alone. It is important to cultivate support by reinforcing your connections with people who see your greatness and want to help you achieve it. Key relationships mean the difference between being good and being great.

Y- Yesterday's mistakes are behind you even if you are still dealing with their consequences. Yesterday cannot be corrected, but today, tomorrow, and next week need your undivided attention and strategy to excel.

SELLS

S- Sincerity matters. As a coach, when I notice people only want to make money in this industry, I decline the client. People feel and are attracted to your sincerity in this industry. I am a firm believer that *impact drives income*. Continue to impact the lives of those around you, and income is inevitable.

LEVERAGE TRANSPARENCY, ACCEPTANCE, AND GROWTH

E- Energy. The greatness you achieve is an expression of powerful energy, fueling the fire that compels you to accomplish at higher and higher levels. One of your big challenges is to maintain winning energy in tough times. So, just act like you are winning. Why? Act the way you want to be, and soon you'll be the way you want to act!

L- Live out loud. Do not shy away from who you are. If you are excited, let the world know. If you are passionate, live your passion daily. Live out your greatness and positive attitude. Let every good thing about you have a ripple effect on those around you.

L- Love yourself and love what you do. It is a simple request, yet so hard to achieve. Loving yourself means not engaging in self-sabotage. Loving yourself means making yourself and your goals a priority. Loving yourself is one of the most important things to master.

S- Sacred space. This space of storytelling, sharing, and transforming lives is sacred ground. Yes, your story sells, but it also heals, delivers, and guides others on their paths to conquer great things. This is a sacred space where you hold the hearts and emotions of those around you. It's where you encourage the downtrodden, illuminate dark places, and find hope in despair. You may be the chosen one to carry this load. It is hard, it is worth it, and it is you. It is possible! This sacred work has your name written on it. Come and pick up your mantle.

You are enough.
You have what it takes.
The world is waiting on your gift.

You heard these words before, but never did you think they applied to you. Now you know they do.

ABOUT LES BROWN

Les Brown is an American motivational speaker, author, and former television host. He is known for his high-energy presentations and his message of personal development and self-improvement.

Born in 1945 in Liberty City, Florida, Les grew up in an impoverished household and was mistakenly deemed Educable Mentally Retarded in primary school. Despite facing numerous challenges and setbacks, he was determined to overcome his circumstances and achieve success. He eventually landed a job as a disc jockey, which led to a career in radio and television.

In the 1980s, Les began working as a motivational speaker, delivering powerful and inspiring messages to audiences around the world. He has written several books, including *Live Your Dreams*, *It's Not Over Until You Win*, and *You've Got to Be Hungry*. His books have been translated into several languages and have sold millions of copies worldwide.

In addition to his work as a speaker and author, Les has also hosted several television shows including *The Les Brown Show* and *The Les Brown Full Throttle Leadership Tour*. He has been recognized for his contributions to the fields of personal development and leadership, receiving numerous awards and accolades throughout his career.

Today, Les continues to inspire and empower people to reach their full potential and live their best lives.

To connect with and learn more about Les, visit lesbrown.com.

Purposeful storytelling isn't show business, it's good business.

— Peter Guber

WEALTH GROWS ON TREES
Jerremy Alexander Newsome

My Story, My Wealth

In 1994, my father and oldest brother were watching a movie. I, being a "thirsty for attention" young boy, made sure to place myself on the brown couch where the adults were watching the winner of the Academy Award for Best Picture for that year.

Do you know the name of the 1994 Academy Award for Best Picture movie?

Forrest Gump.

Forrest Gump changed my life. About eighty-three percent of the way through the film, there is a scene where Forrest begins describing all of his winnings, businesses, and accomplishments. And then at the mailbox he says, "Lieutenant Dan got me invested in some kind of fruit company ... saying we didn't have to worry about money no more. And I said, 'That's good! One less thing.'"

*Well I grew up about thirty minutes south of where Deliverance was filmed in a single wide trailer treehouse type of home. Think mega redneck Swiss Family Robinson style house. Keep in mind, money was definitely something we worried about. In fact, I was unaware that it was an option, choice, or even possibility to never worry about money, **ever again**.*

I was hooked, and I needed more information. Seconds after that line finished, I asked my father, "What is investing and what is the fruit company?"

My dad did his best to tell me about Apple Computers and how investing works, giving me his thoughts and insights on the stock market.

Immediately I began to ask him, maybe even begged him, to buy some shares of Apple, just like Forrest Gump.

He told me this was a movie, this was fiction, and investing was not for poor people like us.

After months of my whining about buying shares of Apple, my dad finally caved in and said, "Look, if you bring me some money, I'll match it dollar for dollar and get you the Apple stocks you want."

That was the trust and conviction I needed to begin to figure out how to invest in the fruit company, Apple, just like Forrest.

You see, it is not about your resources; it is about your resourcefulness! In 1994, I was six years old. I walked up and down my dirt road picking blackberries and selling them to neighbors for a dollar a bag. Thanks to many people overpaying for my bag of berries, I made $1,500 by the summer of 1995.

True to his word, my dad matched my $1,500 (come to find out, he borrowed some money from my uncle), and we bought $3,000 worth of AAPL stock in 1995.

WEALTH GROWS ON TREES

Do you recall what Forrest did with his Apple money?

He built schools, churches, and hospitals, and he helped Bubba's mom retire "so she didn't have to work in nobody's kitchen no mo."

That is the part where my six-year-old soul was elevated and transcended to learn what wealthy, fortunate, abundant individuals do! They give, provide, help, produce, create, organize, establish, and truly assist others. My subconscious latched on powerfully to that version of wealth, and I wanted to create it for my family! So I did.

Keep in mind, this is a real story. This is *the* story I tell when I am on a podcast or on stage. It is essentially my go-to intro of "who I am." I've written about this story at least one hundred times, spoken it on stage in over three hundred instances, and told it during more than four hundred podcasts.

How does my story help me with business?

I created a global stock market education company. My energetic elixir is making sure others understand how easy, simple, fast, efficient, and effective investing can be. It can be done very wrong, and it can be done very right. Just like anything else.

My story is the foundation of who I am, what I believe, and what I know to be true about money and wealth. I was a dirt poor boy from Georgia without a penny in my hand or shoes on my feet, but I had a calling, and I chose to step into that calling regardless of challenging situations and circumstances. I did this because I knew I was to teach people how to have ultimate freedom and peace in their hearts. And then I honed my craft! I learned. I studied. I scripted. I planned. And I put the puzzle pieces together to blend and create a symphony of sales for my business.

The Power of Story

But how did I do it? Through the power of story.

Now, how do you create more cash flow, additional revenue, and excessive wealth through story, you ask? Simply put, share your story—transparently and authentically. Share the good, and share the bad. Share the struggles, and share the lessons learned. The truth is: good stories engage the listener! When we are engaged, we are committed. Commitment builds trust, and trust is *everything* in a relationship. When people trust you, they will buy from you.

I am going to cut to the chase for you. Why should you care about stories and telling them well? Because it will help you make gobs of money.

You are welcome. :-)

When I talk about the power of story to my clients and to audiences worldwide, I'm most often met with sentiments of fear, overwhelm, and doubt: "Who will listen? Who will care? Everyone will think I'm stupid, silly, meaningless, or not interesting." They express fears of being judged in their vulnerability and transparency. And they express overwhelm at the thought of sharing their story because they don't know where or how to start.

Not to worry, in these pages, I am going to show you *exactly* how you can craft your story, speak it, and leverage it to grow your wealth, cash flow, and *finally* become financially free!!

Follow along for my five secrets of powerful storytelling that will make you wealthy!

Secret 1: Use Relatable Elements

This one is easy. Find simple, useful, relatable items or topics of discussion that most listeners can relate to and connect with. *Most* storytellers will start with something radical, wild, or insanely unique to try to capture attention. That *can* work, but only if you've practiced it, and the plot is truly one of a kind.

For the rest of us, consider that we, despite coming from a wide range of backgrounds and possessing unique characteristics, share many more similarities than differences.

There are fundamental behaviors and thought patterns that we all share. These consistent traits appear repeatedly in the stories we tell, making them essential building blocks for any narrative.

Humor is relatable to nearly everyone. I love laughter because it sounds the same in every language. So humor is an element that I successfully weave into my stories.

The beautiful man on the cover of this book (on the left), Les Brown, once told me in a coaching session we shared together: "Everyone had a dad and everyone had a mother." He continued, "Everyone has parents, and chances are if you speak about your mother and father, you will begin to capture the attention of those who are listening, because they will begin to think about their mom and dad."

What was my relatable element in the *Forrest Gump* story? Watching a movie with my family.

Relatability is easy—use it!

Secret 2: Build Curiosity

I recently attended a mastermind and networking event in Vail, Colorado. The man on stage was discussing how to raise capital for a business. My *huge* takeaway was not about raising capital at all. Rather it was about how many storytellers butcher the pivotal component of all stories—the reveal. So many storytellers get it wrong. They fumble around in the beginning of the story and wind up introducing the end!

Even stories that we already know can be successfully reframed to contain a reveal. Remember the movie *Titanic*? You watched it, I watched it, the world watched it. *Titanic* was the #1 best-selling movie at the box office for more than a decade—EVEN THOUGH every single audience member already *knew* the ending. We were all aware the ship sank and people died. That was not a tremendous revelation. So what made the movie so compelling?

It was the love story between Jack and Rose that was intertwined in the drama of the sinking ship. Their relationship held everyone's attention. Everyone was rooting for the love birds to survive, but no one knew if they would!

Every story should create intrigue. The audience should want to know what is going to happen next. Build mystery in a story! Even jokes need to pique your audience's intrigue. What makes a joke funny? The presentation, the pause, and the punchline. A successful joke triggers curiosity!

How did I build curiosity in my *Forrest Gump* story? I built intrigue by saying that I placed myself on the brown couch with my dad and brother. What was going to come of me insisting on joining them for their movie?

Secret 3: Seed Questions

Weaving questions throughout your story to engage the audience is a winning element. Every story should have questions sprinkled in. No one wants a barrage of information. Consider the three components of a story: the known, the unknown, and the hero.

The known are the facts, the relatable aspects to the story, the parts that build familiarity. The unknown is where the questions come in—the intrigue, the curiosity, and the reveal! Lastly, the hero is you, or the audience as your proxy!

Ask questions during your storytelling. I bring the audience into my story by asking them if they know what movie won the Academy Award for Best Picture in 1994. Some might immediately know it was *Forrest Gump*; others might just start thinking through famous movies or some of their favorite movies from that decade. Either way, I have them hooked into my story.

Engage your listener as if it was a personal conversation, and make the listener ponder. Though you'll often speak to groups, asking questions allows each audience member to feel that you are having a direct conversation with them personally. For bonus points, make the questions easy to answer because people love to be right!

Secret 4: Link Your Story and the Listeners' Outcomes

The goal here is beautiful and easy. In every story you spin, the hero should be you or your audience as a proxy of you, which makes it very easy for them to understand the end goal, result, and outcome.

I call this one "know your room." Your tone, language, emphasis, and outcome will change depending on whether you are reading a book to a second-grade class, doing a presentation in front of your boardroom, or perhaps trying to convince your three friends to join you at a specific burger joint.

For example:

If I wanted to visit the best burger spot in Salt Lake City, Utah, I would spin a yarn about how the specific establishment had ... wait for it ... the most delectable burgers and shakes.

I simply repeat that process while visiting a new city to track down another perfect beef patty.

In my *Forrest Gump* story, it's pretty easy for the audience to put themselves in my shoes—maybe not the poor kid from Georgia part, but certainly being struck and influenced by a movie. And we've probably all done simple chores as young kids to earn some money for something that piqued our interest!

Secret 5: Create a Compelling Offer!

A compelling offer is something that *almost* sounds too good to be true. It comes after the customer trusts you because you are being real, open, honest, and transparent. And then that customer buys from you, exchanging their money for your value.

Your story is how you build that trust!

In my *Forrest Gump* story, I use my experience to make a compelling offer to teach my audience the power of investing, the ease of it, and how we should use our surroundings and the inputs of our lives to make meaningful decisions.

I wrote a book called *Money Grows on Trees*. In this book, I discuss how broke I was. I go into depth about my mental self-discovery and the exact routes I took to become more wealthy—the investments I made, the books I read, the affirmations I spoke each day, along with the new beliefs I adopted about wealth and money.

That book is my story. It encapsulates two decades of my life and leads the reader to my website treesaremoney.com where they can explore the next soul-shifting event that transforms the energy and the money frequency of all who attend! That's my compelling offer.

Stories Earn Profit

My wife's business is a perfect example of how personal stories (and of course the underlying struggles and wisdom earned) can generate profit.

She grew up in the country of Kazakhstan, formerly part of the USSR. She came to America for the first time when she was nineteen years old. Her story is one of poverty, struggle, and then overcoming. She had reached a high point and felt on top of the world only to have it all ripped out from under her. She again struggled and worked her absolute hardest for seven years as a single mother—trying, pushing, striving, and ultimately achieving, every single day.

And though she succeeded, her journey was painful. She wanted to save individuals that same pain, and began to question: "Is it time for another way? What if there was ease in this world, simplicity, beauty, and grace without always having to struggle, chase, and pursue?"

She now offers a course in which she teaches and guides her students through a process of dreaming, vision boarding, and manifesting, all done with some extremely specific and concrete rules based on her experiences.

She successfully monetized her story and its outcome and created wealth with it. She charges $1,555 for her course. Over two hundred people have purchased it in the last three years, which is a tad north of $300,000. We have used that money to invest in real estate, flip properties, and grow those proceeds to almost $500,000 now. I believe anyone can do this, with the right story, message, and value associated with it.

Your Story, Your Profit

You know what's cool? You have a lifetime of stories you can use. Your story can be from last year, yesterday, or the fifteen minutes right after you woke up this morning when you had a stark revelation about the softness of pillows being the cause of your neck pain.

So what stories will you tell? Pick one and try it! Just make sure you use the realness, the bitter truth, the no makeup, no filter version of what really happened to capture your audience's attention and create a compelling story.

I personally believe this is the easiest and fastest way to become a liquid millionaire. You sell your story, your pain, and your insight into how others can overcome theirs.

Your story is as important as everyone else's story. You are called to do great things and share your skills, knowledge, and talents with the world. Don't be one of the many people that say, "I always wanted to write a book." Be the person who says, "I wrote a book about ...." Don't be one of the many people that say, "I always wanted to be a speaker." Be the person who says, "I speak about ...." Use the elements I've shared with you to create your compelling story. Then say it, share it, and keep molding it until you have verbalized the story that reflects you—your knowledge, your dreams, your lessons learned, your growth.

Use your honesty and transparency to build trust and relate to your audience and customers. In my public speaking mentorship, The Power of the Pause, I work with people who are passionate about telling their stories with purpose, transparency, style, and efficiency to enrich the lives of others. I create compelling offers, incredible programs, and opportunities to really dive into your essence, your gift, and your skillset to propel you and your family's finances. Maybe you are interested in sales? Public speaking? Day trading? House flipping? Meditation? Active stocks and options trading? Entrepreneurship? Whatever it is, reach out and let's connect. Our journeys will meet, and it will be incredible!

Email me at jerremy@reallifetrading.com to share your story. Be sure to put in the subject line: "Hear my story!" I can't wait to read it and do my best to pour into your life!

You can also reach out to me on any social media. Google my name and you will find ways for us to connect. Because I want you—no I need you—to be the next success story I tell! I look forward to hearing your story and can't wait to witness how your story sells.

ABOUT JERREMY ALEXANDER NEWSOME

Jerremy Alexander Newsome is the founder and CEO of Real Life Trading, a stock market education company that is one of the highest rated customer service companies on the internet. He is considered one of the leading global minds on stock market education and is frequently featured on the Forbes Council.

His mission is to enrich lives with mentally liberating education. Jerremy knocks down barriers and creates a way for everyone to have access to the same tools that have made him wealthy. Because he believes everyone should learn how to be financially free, he offers high quality, free stock trading education. He even has stock trading education programs for young adults and kids ages seven to fourteen!

A world-renowned storyteller with unparalleled energy, wit, and charisma, Jerremy is the co-host of the *Broke to Woke* podcast and is a guest on many others. In addition to leading retreats that deliver massive results for people all over the world, he leads many masterminds and mentorships including The Power of the Pause, TSLA Titans, and Grow, Learn, Develop. He is a lifelong philanthropist and started the Real Life Foundation, a nonprofit organization.

To learn more about Jerremy and how he uses his knowledge and exuberance to be a force for good, visit jerremynewsome.com and reallifetrading.com.

Stories are a communal currency of humanity.

— Tahir Shah

INSPIRED IMPACT
Kate Butler

As your head hits the pillow, I lie next to you and gently rub your back until you float off to dreamland. I stay there just long enough to soak in the smell of your innocence. I begin to think about all the things you will dream about as you sleep, and I begin to dream for you, too. I dream that you will always know how incredibly brilliant you are. I dream that your heart is protected but doesn't harden.

I dream that you are always able to connect to your guidance within so that you may know your way.

I always cherished these quiet moments of nap time. It was a time of solace amidst a normally busy and chaotic day. This was my chance to soak it all in, to take a step back and reflect, even if just for a moment. But today was different. I found myself staying longer than usual in that little pink room. I found myself connecting at a much deeper level and questioning these dreams I was envisioning. The dreams for my children were so clear. But I began to ask myself, "What is your dream for your own life?"

On this day, during nap time in my daughter's room, I found myself next to her bed, on my knees, praying to God. The reality had hit me. It all came crashing down in an instant. This life I had been living was not my dream. It was good. I was blessed. My husband was wonderful and supportive; my children were healthy and beautiful. My home was pretty close to the one I had always envisioned. But I was looking around at this white-picket-fence-life saying, "Now what?" The voice followed up with: "You made a commitment. You made a deal. You are here to *do* more. You are here to give more. You are here to *serve* more."

I picked myself up off the floor and opened my eyes. I could no longer hide behind my busy life or pretend that inner knowing was not there. I knew my time had come.

You see, six years earlier, at the age of twenty-seven, I was diagnosed with a fatal heart condition. By this point in my life, I had successfully worked my way up the corporate ladder. I was running multiple offices as a career, life, and business coach. The offices were yielding millions of dollars in revenue, and I was blessed to be earning well over six figures. It felt like everyone was winning. Along with this high-powered position came a massive amount of responsibility. I was responsible for the operations and P&Ls of multiple offices as well as the livelihood of the employees that worked in those offices. It was a heavy weight to carry, and the stress began to seep into my life. There were signs along the way that I was getting off course, but I refused to see them. This was everything I thought I wanted. I had an amazing career. I was making a lucrative income. My job was centered around helping people. I was certain I was on the right path.

So, when the stress poured in, I did not acknowledge it as a sign that I was off course; I just made a decision that I would handle it like I handled everything else in my life: I pushed harder. I wasn't eating properly, and I wasn't taking care of my body. I simply was not making my well-being a priority. Work was the focus, and there just weren't enough hours in the day for two priorities.

My heart was full of business success, monetary success, and career achievements. But in those quiet moments that were, admittedly, few and far between, I knew there was something missing. My heart was beginning to break for more meaningful work, a life with more balance, and more fulfilling moments.

I started waking up in the middle of the night with panic attacks. I would think, "Did I remember to send that email? Did I ever get back to that client? How am I going to let this person go for not meeting their sales goals?" My mind would race all night long. It was overwhelming and exhausting. I felt like I could not get it under control.

In the mornings, when I was getting ready for work, I would often have to sit down on my bed for several minutes just to catch my breath. I would get myself so worked up over the day's upcoming events that I would find myself breathless.

I would randomly burst into tears for no reason. I would overreact to situations that, rationally, I knew were not a big deal. I found myself in the middle of drama everywhere I turned. I drank too much on the weekends just trying to numb my mind and my emotions. I was spiraling. It all felt like too much. And yet, I felt like this was what I was supposed to be doing. This was the cost I had agreed to pay for the success I had achieved at such a young age. How could I possibly stop now? I couldn't.

And then that fateful Tuesday hit, and it hit hard. I was driving home from work, and I had to pull over to the side of the road. I couldn't breathe. I couldn't speak. I was holding my chest. The pain was excruciating. This was more than a panic attack. This was very different than the stress symptoms I had felt in my body up until that point. This was unbearable.

Over the course of the next few days, I went through a series of doctors' appointments, evaluations, and tests that normally take many months to complete. I knew by the medical professionals' sense of urgency that something was seriously wrong. Within a few days, I was diagnosed with ventricular tachycardia. This basically meant that my heart was beating too much, too fast, and, if not operated on immediately, it was at risk of bursting. This was a fatal condition. Within weeks I was scheduled for surgery.

I was in shock. I was scared. I was uncertain for the first time in a long time. But more than this, I had an inner knowing that this was happening to get my attention. And so I acquiesced.

"I'm ready to listen," I told God.

I began to divinely download His messages. The series of messages He sent me instructed me to get back on course, to connect with my God-given gifts, and that by traveling on my highest path to purpose, I would find true life fulfillment. I took it in and said, "Yes." I made a promise to God that day. If I was graced with a second chance and he was able to fix my broken heart, I would fulfill my mission.

Thankfully, the surgery was a success. Leading up to the surgery, during the surgery, and post-op, every administrator, nurse, doctor, or medical professional that I came into contact with made a production over my age and my stats. They said that there was no indication on my records of anything that would have led to this condition. I was, otherwise, completely healthy. They would bring other doctors in to view my "case." I was an anomaly.

But I knew something they didn't. I knew God was trying to get my attention. I knew that there had been many signs along the way that I could have acknowledged but chose to ignore. And as a result, this was the only way He could get me to pay attention, get me to listen, get me back on my path, and get me back to my life's mission. To me, this all made perfect sense. I was eternally grateful for the breaking and the mending of my heart because now I could clearly see my life's purpose.

Over the next few years, I followed my heart and it led me to love. So much love. I met my handsome husband; we got married, had two beautiful daughters, and settled into our cozy home to begin our life together. My heart was happy. I felt joy and love each day. I did not realize, however, that I had simply replaced one obsession with another: my obsession with work with an obsession for my family. I was pouring my energy, time, heart, and soul into them. It was my greatest joy to do so. But what I did not realize was that in showing up for everyone else, I was once again stepping away from my life's mission. And I had made a commitment.

So, that day in the nursery, when I began dreaming, it all became so crystal clear. There was space for my husband, there was space for my children, there was space for my family and friends, and there was space for my work. But there was also space for my dreams. I was missing a few links of this chain and, in turn, I was not being true to myself or my commitment to God.

With my daughter still napping and this new awareness clearing the fog that had surrounded my life once again, I walked out of my daughter's room, down the stairs, and into my home office. I cleared off my desk and, for the first time in too many years, I gave myself permission to dream again. I began honoring that inner voice that I had been pushing aside. I began tapping into the gifts that I always knew were there. I began putting as much time, energy, heart, and soul into myself as I was putting into everyone and everything else.

I made a second commitment on that day, a commitment to myself. So each day during nap time, I would carve out time to connect with my inner guidance, journal about my future goals, and visualize what these dreams would feel like when they came true.

IGNITE MY FUTURE

I'm so grateful that I now...   6 months ☐   1 year ☐   3 years ☐   5 years ☐

I knew that honoring my inner guidance always led me to experience more joy, but it was also clear to me that I would need to do some more work if I was going to truly understand what my life's mission entailed. Daily meditation was the key element that brought me absolute clarity on my next steps. I still could not see the entire path, but I was certain of the inspired action I was being called to take one step at a time.

IGNITE MY SOUL

My inspired actions consisted of taking full and complete responsibility for my life. I stopped blaming others for my circumstances, and I stopped blaming my circumstances on the things I did not have in my life. Through meditation I began to clearly understand that if I desired something, I had the power to create it. But taking responsibility involved more than that; it was also about seeing the role I played in everything in my life, even the things that were displeasing. This new awareness truly empowered me to begin showing up differently—in every single encounter. With each thought, word, and action, I was literally creating the script for my life.

In addition, I began to notice the miracles that were all around me. Some were small miracles and some giant miracles, but all were equally significant … they were winks from God telling me that I was on the right path. The more I noticed and acknowledged these miracles, the more they occurred, truly proving to me that what we focus on grows.

WINKS & WHISPERS

Ever since I was child, I had been creating vision boards ... actually they were vision books back then. This was before vision boards had a name, before I really knew what I was doing. I felt called to different pictures that captured my dreams, and I would keep them in a book. This process had always proved successful in the past, so I started it again. One vision board became two, and before I knew it, my office walls were covered with images of my dream life. And amazingly, things began to manifest! Some things quickly, other things not in the way that I had expected, but there was no doubt things were changing and shifting. I could *feel* it.

As my way of living began to change, I began to attract more peace, harmony, and happiness into my life. The people around me began to notice and ask what was different. At first, I wasn't sure I could articulate it. But as I became more comfortable with my shift in perspective, I began to share my new awareness and techniques with the women in my life. To my amazement, these women's lives also began to transform before my eyes! Before I knew it, they were referring me to their friends and co-workers, I was hosting retreats and group calls … and from this my coaching practice was born. I went on to become a Certified Professional Success Coach (CPSC), primarily focusing on the intuitive downloads I receive for my clients—most of which have proven to be life changing.

I not only wanted to share this with my clients, I also had a strong desire to teach my children the power of mindset. I began to feel a strong pull to write a children's book. I thought that if I desired to have a book that taught my children how to view life from a new angle, there must be other mothers out there looking for this type of children's book as well. As a result, my idea for my first book was born. I was dreaming again, and I was dreaming big.

I was dreaming big, but still with an infant and toddler in tow. And so now during nap time, I would engage in my daily disciplines. I was continuing to meditate, write my future intentions, and engage my vision board. But I would also spend time taking action toward writing my book, researching printers, and figuring out how I was going to get this book out into the world.

IGNITE MY EXPANSION

Next Level Goal:

1.

2.

3.

Email Ignitor Partner

Once I committed to the dream, the people, circumstances, and resources that I needed effortlessly fell into my lap. I was amazed. In my corporate position, it seemed as if we worked so hard for a sale. We hustled to meet our goals. But this just came so easily.

When I surrendered to the dream of writing an inspirational children's book on the power of a positive perspective, I didn't know anyone who had ever written a book before. I wasn't sure how I would find an editor, an illustrator, or a publisher, but I knew it was something I was being called to do, so I took one inspired action at a time.

My first children's book, *More Than Mud*, was created. And even though I was a novice author, the book took on a life of its own. *More Than Mud* went on to become a #1 international best-selling book and remained on the Amazon bestseller charts for over one hundred consecutive weeks. With the success of this first children's book, I felt inspired to continue. Only this time my daughter Bella was finding her inspiration as well! Bella helped create the story for our second children's book, *More Than Magic*, which had just as much wild success on the bestseller charts. At five years old, Bella became a #1 international best-selling author. And, yup, you guessed it … my daughter Livie went on to follow the same path when she published our book *Believe Big* and followed in the same footsteps and received the same accolades as her mama and older sister.

Our books have been showcased in schools, turned into plays and performances, and have inspired children all over the globe. I believe the success we found was the grace of God for honoring our stories and showing up for our assignment to share our stories to heal and inspire others.

The success of our children's books began to organically create a community of moms who were the people purchasing these books. An inspirational community began, and I started hosting workshops and retreats around the personal growth concepts that I shared in these books. As my coaching grew and our community exploded, I felt like it was time to share my message in a bigger way. I loved reaching children through these books, and I loved coaching the women in our community; however, I decided it was time to write a book with my own personal story in an effort to reach the masses. I am a big believer in the power of collective intention. So, I decided, along with publishing my own story, I would invite other women to publish with me. My belief was that twenty stories would be even more powerful than one. Our book *Women Who Ignite* was born and went on to inspire millions around the globe. Making the decision to share my story with the intention to help, heal, or inspire another soul was a defining moment in my life and business. This book was the start of what is now called the *Inspired Impact Book Series*™. We now have eleven best-selling titles in this series and have published more than three hundred #1 best-selling authors through the books. Sharing my story catapulted my dreams, my business, and my impact, and it also created the platform for others to do the same.

We all have a story, a message, a purpose to share with the world. Our stories are powerful beyond measure. Stories connect us, teach us, inspire us, and propel us forward. Stories help us understand the past, and the story you decide to write will create our future. Make it a good one.

ABOUT KATE BUTLER

Kate Butler is a world-renowned #1 international best-selling author, publisher, speaker, and host of the TV show *Where All Things Are Possible*. She is also the creator of the *Inspired Impact Book Series*™, a #1 international best-selling series that has published over three hundred authors. Kate focuses on taking her clients' stories and bringing them to life in a best-selling book. It's her specialty! Kate guarantees that when publishing with her, your book is guaranteed to be a bestseller.

As a CPSC, Certified Professional Success Coach, she offers dynamic live and digital programs creating transformational experiences to ultimately help clients reach their greatest potential and live out their dreams, including becoming a #1 best-selling author through her mentorship. Kate believes in learning the tools to help create those infinite possibilities in her clients' lives. Her passion is teaching others how to activate their authentic mission and share it for massive impact while also creating a lucrative business.

Kate's expertise has been featured on Fox 29, Good Day Philadelphia, HBO, PHL17, Roku, the RVN network, and many more TV and radio platforms.

To learn more about how you can connect and work with Kate and discover how *your story sells*, please visit her website at katebutlerbooks.com, where you can find her programs, books, and inspirational products.

Stories constitute the single most powerful weapon in a leader's arsenal.

— Dr. Howard Gardner

WHO CAN I CONNECT YOU WITH?
Winnona Gaviglio

Do you enjoy networking events, those organized functions to cultivate business relationships, gain clients, and create further opportunities for yourself? Some people thrive in the environment. But many others find scouring the room looking for people to impress and with whom to develop long-lasting professional relationships to be difficult. For some, it's a welcomed distraction from their actual work while for others, it's an uncomfortable, intimidating, overwhelming, anxiety-laden chore! I was in the latter group. I was scared to attend networking functions because I didn't like talking about myself. I felt inadequate and insecure. When I did actually muster the courage to attend networking functions, I knew that connecting with people required more than simply asking for their business cards, and I struggled to do it. Even when I managed to receive a number of business cards, it abruptly ended there because I never felt confident enough to reach out to them afterwards. Building connections was going nowhere, which meant that I was going nowhere ....

Fear

From early childhood, I held a deep-rooted belief that I wasn't interesting and that people didn't want to talk to me. I was always the youngest in my class and didn't have the social skills needed to adapt to new environments and new people. And as a first-born, I interacted more with adults than other children. I noticed that children who performed well and completed tasks were the ones praised by the teachers. I concluded that to be accepted, I needed to impress adults. So, I vigilantly observed anyone who was around me, trying to figure out how to *Be* with a capital "B." As a child, I believed that status, and therefore safety, was created by connection with authority: "It's not what I know, but who I know and who I am associated with." This set me up to be a lonely people pleaser. I became the teacher's pet and overcompensated for my perceived inadequacies by focusing on impressing others more than self-development and cultivating normal childhood relationships. I was constantly trying to prove that I belonged.

I also struggled to put myself out into the world because of my Western cultural belief that self-focus is hubris. Talking about myself felt like bragging or boasting—something I was taught that we as people, *especially women*, should never do. I had been taught that this was arrogance, and arrogance was reserved for those who looked down on others. How does one talk about themselves while networking when they intrinsically believe it is rude or stuck up to do so? Networking became a vicious cycle: talk about myself and feel like a self-centered person *or* not talk about myself and feel disconnected, different, and inadequate. No matter what, my flawed belief was reinforced: "I am not worth talking to, and I have nothing to offer."

WHO CAN I CONNECT YOU WITH?

Becoming a Marketing Consultant

I took an aptitude test in high school that determined: "You will be a teacher." I wasn't too excited by this result. I redid the test—knowing what the questions would be—and changed my answers to ensure a preferable outcome. Round two and, voilà, the test results were adamant that I should become an actress! I couldn't have been more thrilled. It was short-lived, however, because I didn't want to be a struggling artist. A teacher I became. Truth be told, I chose this path because I could be a teacher anywhere in the country, and it would provide me with job security. I was always searching for safety, always keeping my eye on the harbors of life should I ever be at sea.

Teaching was where my marketing skills began. I had to convince hundreds of children that they had to learn what I was teaching them, and, more importantly, provide adequate motivation for them. Talk about a challenge! But I was good at it. Very good at it. In fact, it unleashed and refined my creativity.

After I had my first child, I left the workforce and abruptly went from being a public school teacher to becoming a full-time, stay-at-home mom. It was amazing to have this time with my children, but there was a simmering restlessness within. Like most mothers, I believe that we are not only mothers. We are artists, entrepreneurs, businesswomen, CEOs, fund managers, real estate tycoons, writers, sports stars, and politicians too. So I began to keep an ear out. I met someone at a children's play center who sold nutritional supplements and invited me to join. I declined at the time but eventually got involved a couple years later.

Selling the products was easy because I could talk about something other than myself. I rationalized, "You never have to fear speaking about yourself if you make sure that you never have to speak about yourself." The nutritional supplement company suggested that I go door to door. While I was good enough at it to sell products, I was unable to recruit people or create and maintain contacts because that required "relationship building." And build a relationship I was unable to do in a mere thirty seconds. As a result, it eventually fizzled out.

Many years later, I took a job at a startup. I was encouraged to branch out and attend events in order to expand and make more sales. Though these networking events had a more intentional goal of selling the company, my fear and anxiety came back a million-fold. I was crippled by a lack of identity. I was a mother of two with limited exposure to the world of business. If someone had checked my credentials and told me my name was "Imposter," I would have believed them. I was losing my confidence, and my networking was going nowhere, which meant that I was going nowhere too. Again.

Making My Move

I needed a new move. I wondered if the buddy system might help me at these events. After all, evolution has shown that there's safety in numbers! When I arrived at my next function, I made a beeline toward the check-in desk and asked the receptionist if they knew of anyone who would be good to talk to and connect with. My plan was to attach myself to one person so that I could relieve some of the burden of starting up conversations. "Genius," I thought. The receptionist kindly pointed out an individual. I introduced myself and made a concerted effort to stick by their side for the remainder of the event. And, sure enough, I found it far easier to meet with and talk to people when I had someone else beside me. It was so easy to introduce and talk about my companion! What started out as me wanting to meet people and promote my business soon became me introducing other people and promoting them. It removed the attention and potential rejection from me. It was an unusual outcome for a networking event, but it seeded an idea. By facilitating introductions between others, I paved the way for many businessmen and businesswomen to forge relationships and grow their businesses. Being a wingwoman and hypewoman for others made them successful, and I found that professionally and personally fulfilling.

Drastic Changes

Unfortunately, my networking buddy strategy came to a screeching halt when COVID-19 hit. No more in-person events meant no more strategy, which meant no more business. Like the rest of the world, I moved online and found a local networking event. There I met a woman from the UK who was trying to promote her coaching business. We connected effortlessly, which was unusual for me. Our connection was refreshing and authentic. We chatted regularly after meeting, five or six times a month from thereon. I spoke about wanting to start my own business and told her about my networking buddy system. She listened attentively and helped me to figure out what my skills were. In exchange, I assisted her with a brochure that she wanted to share with two of her virtual network groups from the US. She explained that she had one shot to make a good first impression, and she knew I had the skills to help her achieve this. She said, "You have the American eyes and the skill to see the glaringly obvious things that should or shouldn't be on the brochure." She believed that I could ensure that her presentation would not feel foreign to the Americans. I helped her frame her offer. I explained that she should change "Our company is going to give you …." to "You're going to get …." to put the focus squarely on her potential clients. Her business was about helping others, and this simple reframing made it more authentic. She had sixteen new people sign up for her program after receiving this brochure, and she never looked back.

She was also on to something about me. She excitedly explained that this facilitation of business relationships is what I should be doing, that I could do it for others too, that I should make it my business! I remember wondering at the time that if a successful business coach was telling me that I had everything I needed to flourish, what was stopping me? Imposter Syndrome 101 was the culprit. I couldn't shake the idea that this was too easy. But my friend responded, "Why would you wanna do something that isn't easy for you?" That hit me right where it needed to. It was as if I had been waiting for the last piece of the puzzle to fall into place, and it just had. She then told me that she had a meeting in the US that she needed to attend but couldn't make it in person, and that she wanted me to represent her instead. Yes, she wanted me to be her networker-for-hire and her boots on the ground. She asked me to prospect for her.

We established such a good relationship because we could speak openly and directly with no filter. We weren't pretending in order to seem palatable or agreeable. Authenticity is the most underrated tool in the modern business world. I decided from that day on that my goal was not to become a salesperson for myself because it wasn't authentic to who I was. I speak better for others than I do for myself, and I have made that skill work for me. I can be me in the best way it serves myself and others, personally and professionally. I am my business, and I am my own product. It is authentic and connected. It is my truth. My story. And it sells.

The Importance of Connections

Think about this for a moment: the restaurant or shops you frequent most are where you will most likely know the waiters, sales people, door people, or chefs. Over time, they have probably come to know the more authentic you too. These kinds of places are our favorites because we are comfortable there, and because even when something goes wrong, it will be remedied. Why? Because the *relationship* you have built with them ensures that it gets sorted out. The relationship comes first. You feel cared for, and you feel connected. People will feel more connected with you too. Any person that has an actual relationship with you is more likely to focus and take care of you. Your story is your vehicle for connection. It is how you build your network. And the networks we build are as important to our lives as the food we eat.

But many people, though they actively pursue relationships, particularly in the professional scope, struggle to build them consistently and well. Having the skills to build a business does not mean having the skills to share or talk about said business in order to market or scale it. And even if you have the skills, it's not always the best use of time.

Let's say that you are a service provider and are looking for events to attend so that you can network and promote your business. You spend weeks sifting through various platforms to find a suitable event to go to. Finally, you find an event that could have some potential clients. You go but spend the majority of the time alone or handing out business cards to anyone who will take them. You know that your business card will end up being stacked amongst hundreds of other business cards. You chat with a few people, but in some cases quickly see that they aren't really a match for your service. But you can't end the conversation abruptly because these same people are trying to promote themselves to you. This consumes valuable time. You return home exhausted, with a stack of business cards, all the while wondering if you made an impact and whether the people you want to call actually will. You've spent money on flights and accommodation, and you can't help but contemplate whether it was all worth it. The next day you're back running your business feeling more uncertain than ever before.

Putting It All Together

What if you could hire a professional who could do this for you? A professional who could share your story with others and bring you prospects. Imagine getting someone else to do the uncomfortable work you don't enjoy doing, or that you don't have the bandwidth to do well? That's where I come in! I will set up an hour-long meeting with you to learn about your goals, how you would like to grow, and what you see yourself doing going forward, as well as gather some testimonials and stories that will best position me to connect and promote your business or service. An hour only? Yes! Experience has taught me that having too much information sets me up to "unload," and I have no intention of unloading. My intention is simply to share your story, because your story sells. My goal is always to connect with prospects and create interest about who you are and what you do so that you can do the rest.

I'm all too aware that time is the most precious commodity, and I'm grateful that my clients hire me to maximize theirs! After our initial hour-long conversation, I get busy doing all the groundwork and research for events, expos, and in-person meetings where your target audience or vendors will be. I go and market and promote your service or your business, so you don't have to. It's as simple as that. And I ensure that I know walking in the door exactly who to speak to at the chosen event. I spend most of the event in front of the right people sharing your story and promoting your product or service in the best way possible to successfully connect and achieve my goals. Or your goals I should say! I also use effective tags or hooks that open the door to follow up and refer. Sharing your story and your business is all done in a way that prevents me from coming across as a salesperson pushing your product, service, or business. Instead, I come across as a well-connected and talented networker who is extremely helpful to them and others. People I connect with at events end up thanking me for assisting them but don't really know that this was what I was paid to do.

In the end, my expertise at sharing your story with the right prospects for your business allows you to use your time to do what you need to without any additional stress or worry. You can focus on what best serves and aligns your goals and puts you in the best position to scale and grow your business without having to do the sometimes very uncomfortable and time-consuming work of prospecting. Once I have networked for you, I will touch base with you to explain who I connected with, what was discussed, and what the potential clients' interests or needs are so that you can prepare and better position yourself to convert during the follow up. This positions you to have all the right strategies and solutions ready when you meet with them, enabling you to close the deal with greater efficiency and ease. So, tell me, who can I connect you with?

ABOUT WINNONA GAVIGLIO

Winnona Gaviglio has always been involved in some form of marketing. Whether selling cupcakes to tourists, cookware and cooking services to Californians, supplements and transportation services to Hollywood, or digital marketing to potential prospects, Winnona is known for her creativity and ability to understand just what people need. She even "sold" ideas to her students when she taught middle school language arts in Los Angeles! There she focused on developing her students' skills in reading, writing, and speaking—fundamentals that would later serve her in teaching entrepreneurs how to develop, communicate, and sell *their* ideas.

Winnona uses her passion, creativity, and ingenuity to foster innovative marketing solutions that convert. A master networker, she has spent a lifetime honing her skills and delights in using them to cultivate opportunities for her clients.

Known for her high conversion rates and high close rates, Winnona is regularly asked to join or train organizational sales teams. She founded Link Executive, Inc. to teach business owners around the globe how to develop and communicate their messages, missions, and visions in ways that connect, convert, and close.

Winnona spends her free time singing at karaoke bars, dancing at salsa clubs, growing tomatoes in her garden, volunteering, and taking her two daughters to museums and concerts. On days ending in *y*, she will break into a song that is relevant to that day's adventures. Winnona's hidden talent is transforming a traditional meal into a completely vegan concoction that still tastes delicious.

To connect with Winnona or learn more about her work, visit uktousamarketing.com.

After nourishment, shelter and companionship, stories are the thing we need most in the world.

— Philip Pullman

MY IDENTITY, MY DESTINY
David Grace

My Story

Like most people in Africa, I was born into poverty. Not average poverty, abject poverty. Not the at-least-we-could-afford-a-square-meal type of poverty, but the type of poverty that made me question the reason for my existence. I asked my mum the hard questions and questioned God's integrity in dealing with everyone fairly. I was aggressive, defeatist, and very self-destructive. I blamed my father for most of my childhood misfortune. I felt that if it were not for his cowardice in abandoning my mother, I could have had a much better life. My mother had to raise the six of us on her own. I also clung to the idea that being born in a first-world country could have changed my odds a million-fold. Instead, I directly witnessed the brutal impact of poverty on my life and those around me. How could we eat the food we ate and call ourselves normal, let alone be satisfied? How could we wear the clothes we wore and cultivate or maintain any form of self-respect or self-esteem?

I was still in elementary school when my mind was made up. I wanted to be noticed, I wanted to be somebody whom people would talk about, and I wanted power. Becoming a hardened criminal was the way. I had seen criminals and what they had in comparison to the average person, and I wanted the same. A wounded part of me looked forward to living a life of instilling fear in others and demanding respect because I was the one who lived in fear and was constantly disrespected. I had a darker complexion compared to most of my peers, and they made fun of my color. I was shamed, called names, and constantly harassed by bullies on the playground. Even playing soccer, I was rejected; I was told that my color would bring bad luck (how this could be still eludes me) and that I was not welcome. I struggled academically too. In a class of forty, I was in the bottom three. The academic failure and name calling from teachers and students made me hate school. Most days, I would leave home dressed for school, but would spend the day at the river returning in the evening to be greeted by my mum's stinging cane. I didn't care about this or anything else, and it was evident that I was going nowhere fast.

My brother loved reading. He had a book collection of mostly American cowboy novels and history books. I was around the age of twelve when he started pestering me to read some of his books. My teacher that year was just as obsessed with books as my brother was. On the first day of her arrival, she asked me for my school books, but I had none. I had used most of them for toilet paper in our pit latrine at home. She gave me a thorough beating and told me that I was not dumb, just plain naughty. Before she had arrived at the school, all students who struggled academically were placed at Table E and Table F at the rear of the classroom. She, however, moved me and the rest of my crew to the front. And, she paid attention to us. She saw us and made us feel like we deserved to be in that classroom as much as any of the other children. In tandem, my teacher and brother instilled in me the joy of reading, and I embarked on the rigorous journey that only reading can offer. Time flew and before I knew it, I had finished my brother's entire book collection and found myself at the public library.

That same year, I shifted from Table F to Table B, and by the following year, I finally moved to Table A.

Reading books turned my life around. I began to understand almost everything I was taught in class and started to enjoy attending school again. The circumstances at home never changed, but my life at the time did. I discovered a whole new world. Through books, I traveled many journeys without ever leaving my mother's hut. I read a wide range of books that permeated my mind with new possibilities and hope. They revealed that it was possible to escape my current predicament. A new mindset formed within me. Books became my companions. There were times my classmates gathered around me as I read stories from the novels. I became a powerful storyteller. We had no television nor electricity in my mother's hut, yet I was surrounded by the kids who did, as I beautifully narrated the stories of the Wild West.

Life in the village, however, remained difficult for many years, and I got involved with some toxic people. I became a "runner" or "mule" for some local gangsters. A man would give me a concealed package and send me on my way. I once arrived at a destination only to receive a slap on the face and be dispossessed of the given package. I went back to the man, worried I had made a massive error only to be met with a laugh and then handed some money. I was confused and scared, but I got paid so I didn't dwell on it. My behavior had gone wild. I was already smoking and drinking alcohol and would be lying if I didn't admit that the life I was living was a godless one. This carried on until I was seventeen ... until something remarkable happened to me one day. I had been on a drinking spree one weekend. When I arrived home from the bar, I went over to my aunt's unfinished hut to get some sleep and find relief from a throbbing hangover. I was fast asleep when I woke up to a strange voice that had called my name. I was ready to slap whoever had decided to disturb me. Realizing there was no one there, I quickly went back to sleep. The voice called my name again. I again woke up, frustrated, but there was still no one there. It was only after the third time my name had been called that I felt compelled to respond. The voice answered back with a clear instruction that it was time for me to go to church. I asked which church because there were none that I knew of, and I was simply told to go to the community center that Sunday. I was also told that I would meet people there who would tell me what to do. I sobered up on the spot and was shaking to my core. My life as it was began to flash before me as if projected onto a television screen. This was the first time I felt the urge to move away from the dangerous life I was living.

I got up and took the only clothes I had and prepared our coal iron to press them. My mother asked me where I was going, and I told her I was preparing to go to church the next day. My mother, who was probably shocked and relieved, responded, "Finally, the devil is going to church!" It broke my heart to realize that my mother had thought of me in this way, but she wasn't far off the mark. I remember weeping about this, and I know in the depths of my heart that if it was not for that day, I would either be dead or incarcerated. I was involved with the wrong company, and my life path was set before me: to be a hardcore criminal. I was an angry young man, and my anger was blind and dangerous. During fits of rage, I would punch a tree in the middle of our yard with my fist until it was torn and covered in blood in an attempt to pacify myself. What happened that day in my aunt's hut was God's divine intervention.

I was the first to arrive at the community center that Sunday. I was still puzzled that the voice had told me that there was a church there because I knew that the place was a club on Fridays and Saturdays. It was still littered with beer cans and cigarette butts, and a young man was passed out in the hall for heaven's sake! I thought this must be a joke, but for the first time in my life, I remember the smell of beer mixed with smoke from a cigarette was repulsive to me. At exactly 9:00 am, the pastor's wife entered the hall singing. She picked up the broom and began to clean up the place, and I found myself with a broom in my hands helping her. This was unlike me, and I worried that I was becoming "soft." The voice that spoke to me had charmed me.

The church had less than twenty members, but there in that place, in April 1999, my life was transformed. The pastor made the call to surrender to Jesus. I went forward without thinking. I prayed, and a new person was born. A new me, one that I never imagined I could be in a thousand lives. A person totally opposite of who I wanted to be. My entire perspective shifted that day. The way I saw life and related with others changed for good. Selfishness was replaced with selflessness. I discovered that I am a child of a King, and armed with this new identity, I knew that I could not settle for mediocrity any longer. It is true that the place of someone's birth can either limit or enhance their potential, and before I entered the door of that church, I was battling with low self-esteem, emotional trauma, and an unending existential crisis.

My faith became my redemption from self-sabotage and self-limiting thoughts. I was full of fear and uncertainty about my future, but as I listened to the teachings in the church, I learned about a God who loves me. The concept of being loved was foreign, and I struggled with it. Far more than being logically understood, I discovered that this love must be experienced. Only once I *felt* this unconditional love was I able to give selflessly to others. I became a generous person, and I continued to learn how God loved me and gave His only Son for me. I began to understand the power of giving.

The principle of being a student of life was also cemented in this church. This is where my journey of personal development started. I was introduced to the books of John Maxwell, Myles Munroe, T.D. Jakes, and many other outstanding faith leaders. They played a pivotal role in the discovery of my purpose in life. As a young man in a small village in my country, I began to see the real possibility of speaking to people all over the world. I saw a picture a billion times bigger than where I originally was. I was dreaming big. A wise man once said that true vision will always be bigger than where you are. I remember an evening where an elder in the church taught the story of Joseph. I was in tears throughout. Could I be the one sent to liberate my family from the shackles of poverty? The elder took us through the journey of Joseph's life. I was shocked at the similarities. How can someone who lived thousands of years ago have a story so remarkable it affected my life that day? I had dreamed of greatness. I shared my dream with those around me and, as was to be expected, many laughed at me, but a few believed. I was saying things that had never been heard before in that environment. The naysayers questioned me: "How could a boy who has never even been to the city utter such things?" I told people that I would be rich, I would hire many people, I would have a great church, and that I would raise influencers! John Maxwell's book *Talent Is Not Enough* became a manual of living during my youth. I became the first person in my family to attend university. I spent my days there with access to electricity and surrounded by thousands of books. I even studied books outside the degree I was pursuing. I was living the words of David Oyedepo: "Every committed reader is a potential leader, and every leading leader is a committed reader." In all my years at university, I dedicated myself to improving my communication, public speaking, and leadership abilities. I appeared in newspapers, and my motivation and inspirational talks were creating waves. I influenced thousands of students in my university and at other institutions around the country. Many of the students who joined me on Friday nights each week for training during my university days now hold elite executive positions in their respective organizations.

This is how I found my true calling. I have dedicated thousands of hours to training young people in my country. Today, I run Destiny Club, a country-wide student hub that offers thousands of students personal development programs. Destiny Club helps produce graduates who have the soft skills to supplement their education, which is vitally important for young adults. I want to build the sort of foundation that goes beyond ordinary schooling—one that creates the possibility of exploring talents beyond academics. I set out to teach young people about the power of using character, attitude, relationships, choices, and critical principles to govern a successful life. Success is not measured by comparing yourself with others but by fulfilling your own purpose in life. I believe that your primary motive in life must be motivated by your purpose. Teaching students that they are going to succeed through academic achievement alone is a mistake, and I aim to point young people in the direction of something more critical. Purpose.

Purpose will determine who becomes their teachers and mentors. Mentors are important because they guide us to operate in a space that is purpose-driven. We learn better in the area of our purpose. I teach young people to understand that if you discover your strength, you will discover the significant role you will have in other people's lives. True education is both formal and informal. It helps you discover your gift and talents and enhance them. You are born with a gift, and the best way to learn how to use it is through those who have successfully used theirs. Mike Murdock once said there is always someone who is where you want to be. No matter what the gift is, someone in the world already has it, and they are using it. *Strategic learning is identifying the mentors of your gift.* Pursue and find what you already have within you, and God will place in your path the people that can mentor you to success.

Inspiring Stories from My Mentors

Fifteen years ago, I met an exceptional God-sent pastor who became one of my mentors. His name is Korede Komaiya, but I call him pastor K.K. I met K.K. during my third year of university, and he took me under his wing. He became a mentor but, in many ways, filled the gap of my absent father. I knew that I wanted to start a church organization, but I needed training. He taught me everything I know about church ministry today. I also knew that I had a unique vision which did not fit into the traditional setup of the church. Rather, I wanted an organization that would be a "university of life." I shared my vision, and he marked out the way. And my vision became reality.

My church is aimed at "unchurched" people in our community. It has a mandate to touch the seven spheres of influence in society: religion, education, family, arts/entertainment, media, business, and government/leadership. When we started this organization, my wife and I knew exactly where we were headed. Today this vision has taken me to unconventional places to speak to people who would never ordinarily enter a church. These people have told me that they often thought that God had no interest in them.

When I share my story about where God has taken me, it feels like I am talking about someone else. After delivering a speech in front of the president of my country, he even questioned if I was a foreigner because he had never seen one of his own countrymen deliver such inspiring leadership before. I have addressed many cabinet ministers from my country and neighboring countries since then. Our organization has reached thousands of people around the world and I, at one point, addressed over twenty thousand people in a single gathering. The transformation I have seen and been a part of in the lives of people has been remarkable. I once set up a branch of our organization to reach people in a particular part of our country. The results were astonishing. Within a year, the crime rate went down to almost zero with some of the most notorious taverns closing down in that area. Even the most feared cattle thief turned his life over to God. The police there could see the clear results of our interventions and involvement through the teachings we offered. Results like this remind me that there is power in every story.

Another of my mentors is Myles Munroe. I have followed Myles religiously for most of my adult life. Once, he spoke of a time when he had just started to coach and consult for organizations, and one of the companies had requested his fee quote. He struggled to come up with a figure that he felt was fair, so he reached out to his friend Les Brown. Les simply told him that if Myles charged anything less than Les's fee, that he would be extremely disappointed in him because Les believed that Myles was even better than he was. You see, God placed Les in Myles's life for times like this. He pushed Myles to not undervalue himself. Myles trusted Les, sent the quote, and was shocked when payment was received the very next day. I remember this story vividly because I experienced the very same thing. I had gone to Orlando to become a certified John Maxwell speaker, teacher, and trainer. When I returned, just like Myles, I struggled to charge organizations a decent fee. I knew I was good, well equipped, and that I got results, but I could not break the idea of charging people more than a few dollars. Yet, I was discouraged to see higher-paid speakers struggle to deliver results. Eventually, I followed Les's advice to Myles, and my life radically improved. I began to read and listen to the legend that is Les Brown daily. His teachings aligned with what I already believed to be true. If formal education becomes the only yardstick for success, then humanity will be robbed of a gift. Les is not schooled, he is educated. He has continuously developed himself and has earned his place among the stars.

After some time, I had built a business from the ground up using the lessons I had learned and the connections I had made, but then it all came crashing down. I had made a bad investment decision, and it ended up costing me everything. I was homeless and in debt. I could not even afford food for my family. The sheriffs attached all my possessions in order to settle my many debts. The calls from people I owed money to were relentless, and it became unbearable to have a phone. My temporary accommodation owner gave me two weeks' notice to leave. I had no idea where I was going to take my family or what I was going to feed them. My heart ached for my young wife and children. They deserved better, but I was stuck. I was truly down and out. I was devastated and suicidal. But I had purchased a new lesson from Les, and decided to take a listen. That lesson laid the foundation for what was to happen next. Les said, "Some of you may be parked in life or parked by the roadside of life. Some of you may even be parked in the dark without hazard lights on, but it is not over. It is not over until you win." I did not sleep that night, and in the morning, I felt ready to win again. I explained to my wife that we were going to build our own house on one of the remaining vacant plots we owned. I had no money, but I humbly asked people for help to clear the site. These people were really kind to share their time with me, and to this day I am extremely grateful. I drew the plans for a two-bedroom apartment. When asked where I was going to get the building materials, I told people about Abraham's story in the Bible, and that "God will provide." I told them we didn't need bricks to start, we needed only to dig the trenches and set the foundation. The fire of Elijah never fell until he prepared the altar, and I was preparing mine. I told them that we should do what man can do, and let God do what God does. The trench had just been completed when a couple I knew passed by and asked me what I was doing. I shared my vision with them. They replied that they had a lot of leftover materials from a large project they had recently completed and wanted to bless us. *What?* I couldn't believe it. With as much emotion as you can imagine, I gratefully accepted. Life is all about the relationships we create through the people we serve. Les Brown revived my dreams, and from that moment on, I knew that what I was going through was not the last chapter in my life. I rose to face my destiny with renewed strength. I finished building that house one brick at a time.

I became a homeowner, gained a mentor in Les Brown, and told my wife that I would meet this man soon. God would set the appointment and I would meet Les one day. I immersed myself into his teachings during the COVID-19 lockdown. I knew my mind needed sharpening, and I desired to learn more from Les. And, ultimately, it manifested into this very opportunity to share our stories by writing a book together.

The Importance of Stories

Stories are meant for others. Your life experience can change someone else's life. And there will always be people somewhere willing to hear you speak, and maybe even pay you for it. You may think there are already enough famous speakers around the world, but if you think they are reaching all the people on earth, you would be wrong. There is a place for your story. There are qualities about you that can bring a change in someone's life, family, business, and possibly an entire nation. The most important aspect is knowing how to use your own story at every level of your life to inspire others. There is power in your story. When you value your story, you value your assignment in the lives of others, and you will never really know which part of your story is powerful to another person until you share it.

My Essential Story

1. Your background is not your future.

2. You have a God-given gift that gives you space in this world.

3. Discover your gift.

4. Educate and enhance your gift, read books, and attend classes, workshops, webinars, and whatever else will help you to improve your ability to express your gift.

5. Use your gift and pursue your vision with the understanding that there are fundamental principles you will discover and learn to use in order to achieve your dream:
   - It is a process, and this process will take time.
   - You are not going to have all the principles all at once.
   - Growth is inevitable, and this will be revealed through both experience and inexperience.

- Success will only show you what you are doing right.
- Failure reveals where you need to grow and improve. You only ever fail when you give up.

6. You cannot make it without relationships. Relationships are critical in this life because you cannot do it alone. So:
    - Find a Mentor
        - There is no such thing as self-made success.
        - We are all, to a degree, dependent on others to succeed.
        - It is your duty to find your mentors. They are available everywhere, and your gift should help you determine who they should be.
        - You must be genuinely inspired by your mentor.
        - You must be open-minded and cultivate a heart to learn from them.
        - Don't fight what you need in life; change will require sacrifice so expect it and embrace it.
        - Pay attention to their stories because therein lie the secrets.

    - Relate with Your Peers
        - Surround yourself with those who understand and encourage your vision.
        - Only relate to those who show commitment and have results.
        - Connect with those who complement your gift. Every gift aligns with a group of like-minded individuals. Artistic people should seek out people who write, paint, act, sing, etc. Businesspeople should seek out people with successful businesses and entrepreneurs.

    - Pay It Forward
        - As you grow and achieve your vision, it is important to give back. The more you share and teach, the more vigilant you'll remain in the principles you follow and share with others.

We should all be students who hunger for knowledge and teachers who give to those who share the same hunger. There will always be people who were once where you were and want to get to where you are now. Sow seeds of knowledge and inspiration into their lives the same way you received them into yours—by sharing your story.

ABOUT DAVID GRACE

David Grace was born and raised in the southern African country of Botswana. There, he founded Kingdom International Embassy, a church organization that inspires the collective and restores dignity to the lives of many who were born into disadvantaged environments. Kingdom International Embassy advocates for the establishment and rebuilding of local community culture and aims to empower individuals and organizations to be centers of influence.

As the managing director of Results Driven International, a training and coaching company, David advises private, parastatal, and government agencies in his home country. He also offers executive coaching to the C-suites of major corporations in Botswana. Additionally, David is the founder and patron of Destiny Club, a leadership and mentorship program that offers personal development training for university students.

David is a highly-sought-after speaker, trainer, and executive coach and has been featured in different media platforms. He has also been recognized for his song writing, singing, and production of inspirational and contemporary gospel music.

David spends his downtime on his farm with his family or exploring the arts, cultural, and historic tourist destinations of Botswana. He is a philanthropist who is driven to be a force for good in the world. To connect with David, visit coachdavidgrace.com.

I'm writing
my story
so that others
might see
fragments of
themselves.

— Lena Waithe

THE PAIN WAS THE PATH ALL ALONG
Nafsheen Luhar

Our task is not to seek for love, but merely to seek and find all the barriers within ourselves that we have built against it.
~ Rumi

I was four years old, and we were at a family gathering. While my parents entertained the guests, a trusted family member grabbed my hand with a firm grip; he was breathing heavily, and his breath smelled funny (alcohol, I later learned). He led me into a dark room. This was the start of eight years of abuse and molestation that led to several more years of self-harm. During this time, food became my companion. It resulted in severe weight gain, and yet, that weight felt like an added layer of protection. Nevertheless, I was judged and made fun of. I became disruptive, withdrawn, and had learning disabilities. My haven, food, became a prison—one I would not leave for many decades, but at least I felt safe there.

My particular wounding pattern—the culmination of emotions that repeatedly get triggered within us when any trauma arises—is "I am a fat, abandoned, unworthy victim." I believed this about myself the majority of my life, and lived in my prison of self-abuse and self-punishment.

The molestation stopped one day when I was twelve years old. It stopped because I saw Oprah Winfrey's TV episode on sexual abuse. For the first time I realized that what was happening to me was wrong. It had never felt right, but suddenly, my instincts that it was wrong were validated. I stayed away from my abuser from this point on. He became fearful of me and what I might say, aware that something in me had shifted. He actually tried to blame me for what he had done and even threatened to harm me and my family if I told anyone. As a girl who had been taught through abuse that men have all the power, I believed him.

By the time I was fourteen years old—alone, miserable in my skin, longing to be heard, seen, and understood—I started to mutilate myself through cutting. I was lost, carrying around the weight of the secret of my abuse. Alone, with no one to speak to, I was unable to process and deal with the pain I felt in every cell in my body. I was desperate to see the unexpressed pain trapped within me released with every blade I drew across my skin ... to feel the excruciating pain from the hot water in the shower on my exposed wounds on my arms and legs ... to wail as they burned and throbbed. That physical pain helped me survive the emotional pain. It helped me release the internal emotional trauma and express the shame and guilt I felt. It was something I could control, something that made sense to me.

I stopped self-mutilating at seventeen when I was almost caught by my beloved father. He asked about my "scratches," and I told him they had been caused by one of our many cats. He must have taken my word for it because that was the end of the matter. I did not want to get caught. I did not want to have to talk about why I carved my screams into my arms. I did not want to have to voice my shame. I did not want to bring attention to myself. I was suffering in silence, and the last thing I wanted to do was bring my shame onto my family. And that was enough to immediately stop.

My dad passed away suddenly in 1998. His death triggered my fears of abandonment, which started when I was five years old when my family accidentally left me at the ocean. I was swimming in the sea on a trip to the beach with my family when a rip tide sucked me out into the ocean. My foot got stuck in the sand, and huge waves washed over me as I was suffocated and gasped for air. I was eventually spat back out to shore, and I ran and sat on some nearby steps. I was safe but shaking to the bone. When I calmed down, I realized that my family had left the beach while I was in the ocean. My parents thought I was with my sisters, and my sisters thought I was with my parents. It was midnight before my family finally found me on that beach. It took them almost an entire day to realize that I was missing, which broke my already wounded heart. Again, I felt like a fat, abandoned, unworthy victim. I avoided the water until I was in my thirties when I finally learned how to swim.

After my dad's death, my mum, sister, and I moved from our home in Kenya to California to live with my grandparents, who did not accept me. Like my peers, my extended family made fun of my body. Beauty in my culture is seen only in those who are thin and light-skinned. I was interrogated, "How did you allow yourself to put on so much weight?" To this day, I'm shocked at how many people in my family took issue with my weight (and not because they were concerned for my health). Every birthday, without fail, I would receive at least one book on dieting from some family member. It hurt to not be accepted by outsiders, but it crushed me to be rejected by my own family. I hated myself for not being thinner, prettier, more acceptable. I hated myself for being difficult to love. I carried this trauma in my mutilated body, so bent out of shape from all the ways I had tried to make myself disappear. The spiral of emotional eating continued, and my weight kept rising as I tried to fill the void. I carried not only the burden of trauma but the punishment I inflicted on myself because of it as well. And once again, I started doing everything for everyone else to gain acceptance and love. I continued to live in a shadow encapsulated by the darkness.

Shortly after we moved to California, my sister got married and moved out. It was just me and my mum from thereon, and it became my responsibility to find a way to provide for us. I have been taking care of her ever since. My dad was an unconventional Indian, Muslim father. While most fathers in my culture worried about getting their daughters married, my dad insisted that his daughters be well educated. He wanted me to be a doctor, and I had volunteered at a hospital one summer vacation to impress him. At the first sight of blood, I knew it was not for me. But I was determined to pursue something, finish my education, and make my dad proud. I knew that he could see and feel me from wherever he was. I picked graphic design because my dad used to design logos back in Kenya, so I thought this would be a connection to him.

I had to take a black and white film photography class as a prerequisite to graphic design. And I fell in love with it! Every time I saw an image appear out of nowhere on my photo paper in the darkroom was a moment of sheer magic that connected to my soul. My dad was also a photographer and loved taking images of kids, African wildlife, and cloud formations. I instantly connected with my dad's love for photography and decided that I had to do a double major. Photography fed my soul like nothing had before. In the calm and meditative darkroom, I was connected to nothing outside of me and united to everything within. I felt like my dad lived through me in these moments. There I was, nineteen years old, severely obese, no self-esteem, no identity, no voice, no sense of self, no desire for learning. And yet I was pursuing a double major and had unexpectedly found something that lit a spark in my soul, something that would later become a vehicle to serve my larger purpose in this world.

Though juggling two majors heavy on physical projects was difficult, I did complete both degrees in design and photography. My college years were also when I first started to challenge my fears of abandonment. My first day of college, the start of the spring semester of 1999, was January 18, a dark, gloomy, ice-cold winter morning. My cousin dropped me off at the steps leading up to the college entrance. Nervous and anxious, I made it up the steps with every ounce of courage I had. But that was all the courage I would have that day. With an ocean of students and teachers running from place to place trying to make it to their classes on time, the hustle and bustle of the first day, and so much chaos and commotion all around, I had no idea what to do and where to go to find my classes. I had no knowledge of how to read the college map that said "You Are Here" or how to follow where to go next. I did not have an ounce of courage to open my mouth and ask anyone for help. No one was coming to my rescue, and I knew it. I felt it in every single cell in my body. I was alone.

I felt lost, insignificant, abandoned, and unworthy (the fat, unworthy, abandoned victim). From 8:00 am until 5:00 pm, I sat on those steps in complete paralysis until my cousin came to pick me up. But the next day, I mustered up the courage to ask for help. And that day will always be significant as my first memorable act toward finding my voice, my identity, and most importantly, my independence.

I graduated in 2006 at the age of twenty-six. But I was at my heaviest weight, around 370 pounds. I had definitely abused my body during college. I slept just three to four hours each night. I ate only one huge meal at the end of the day and bought Starbucks in the morning. And I trudged all my weight plus 30 to 50 pounds of additional photography equipment and design portfolios across campus each day. I remember one day my pulse was racing, I was sweating profusely, I went pale, my left arm was hurting, and my chest ached. I thought I was having a heart attack and called the ambulance only to find out that it was a panic attack due to all the stress I was putting on myself and my body. For the longest time, I hated that 370-pound girl. I hated her so much because I thought she was good for nothing and unworthy. But now, when I look back on these days, I am in complete awe and admiration of her because she was so darn strong and resilient. She made it work despite everything that was against her. And she did it alone. I now have compassion, love, and tremendous gratitude for her, her gentle resilient spirit that was finding a way to survive, and her body that continued to relentlessly support her and show up for her.

After graduating, I applied for many graphic design jobs in and around Sacramento; I even took a shot and applied for a job at Apple. I felt like a pigeon amongst the eight thousand cats salivating for the job. I did not for a single second believe that I had a chance, and yet, they chose me! I was one of eleven people given a job on the spot. I was then able to buy a house and comfortably take care of my mum. It didn't take me too long to get comfortable at work either because I loved what I was doing, I was grateful to have an income, and I was grateful for my independence. I tried online dating for a while because it felt safe. I could keep my distance while forming connections at my pace and on my terms. But I still struggled with shame and felt like I didn't belong in my skin. I realized that I wanted to do something about my weight.

At age thirty-two, I weighed around 350 pounds. But it wasn't just weight I carried, it was years of pain and years of self loathing. A friend of mine at Apple, who had a very successful weight loss journey, put me in touch with her trainer, Tots. My resilience and determination to live and fight for my life had called forth Tots who was one of the most amazing human beings I have ever met. She not only helped me to shed weight, but she guided me to shed links in the chain of my past to finally start to reclaim myself. Somewhere I had lost the heart of the child who was Nafsheen before the pain, the soul who had glittered with possibility and hope. I was starting to remember who she was through the eyes of Tots.

Tots was all about the biggest-dream-you-could-ever-possibly-dream dream. At the time I met Tots, I wore dark clothing as though I was in eternal mourning. Tots taught me to wear colors. She taught me that giving up was not an option. I am here today and doing what I do because she taught me that I am worth it and that I am allowed to dream my biggest dream. I hope that every Nafsheen has a Tots in their life. She taught me that saying no was ok. Tots used to come to train me at 4:30 am in the middle of winter—and she lived about thirty minutes away from me! I told myself, "If a total stranger can wake up at that hour and come show up for you, you have no reason not to show up for yourself."

We did five-mile jogs, which progressed to ten miles and half marathons. I felt like a 300-pound athlete. Tots introduced me to boxing which made me feel truly alive and powerful and connected me to the warrior and the fighter inside. When I boxed, I was in a real fight, a fight for my life. I released trauma, pain, anger, and frustration and discovered my fighter spirit that I never knew existed. To this day, boxing is my favorite way to move my body, connect with myself, let go of what isn't serving me—and it makes me feel like a complete badass!

Weight loss was slow and steady, and I welcomed the results, but the validation and affirmation were what intoxicated me. I still sought the approval of others; this time it just so happened to be Tots. So, I worked on myself but not from love and sovereignty; it was from self-hate and wanting to fit in. I realized that I was still abusing my body, just in a different way. I worked out for six hours a day, I took five daily doses of diet tea, and binge eating and purging came soon after. The physical results came, but at a cost of again dissociating from my body. No amount of exercise, dieting, colors, or dreams could fix what actually needed fixing. I was empty and unfulfilled. I was still a nonentity.

Moment of Truth

In 2015, I was diagnosed with uterine cancer. I underwent treatment for six months and was in remission for another six months only for the cancer to return. This was a moment of awakening for me. I had to wait six weeks for the surgery to remove my uterus, but they would not know what stage my cancer was at until I was under the knife. I made myself extremely sick thinking, "This is it … I will die with nothing to show for my life. I have done nothing to be proud of." This thought was relentless and intrusive. And then one day, I heard a voice crying from within. It was the voice of every cell in my body screaming, "I just need you to love me!" That was the moment I realized that the pain I was in, the cancer that I carried in my body, and how trapped I felt within myself, was all because of my own self-hatred and self-created prison.

With the epiphany I had that day, I vowed to love myself and my body no matter what was to come. I would take care of it with every ounce of my being. I was exhausted from all the years of fighting against myself, of trying to make myself into something I wasn't, of trying to kill myself. I caressed my womb, soothing myself like a child. I believed without a doubt that everything would be fine once I had the surgery. For the first time in my life, I felt content. I also promised myself that I would use what had been revealed to me to heal others through my art and creativity. The way forward was suddenly clear.

Post-Cancer Healing and Learning

For three years prior to my cancer diagnosis I had been dealing with a repetitive strain injury to my right elbow from typing at work. I took a leave of absence from Apple for about a year as I was terrified that I would never be able to paint again—a creator's worst nightmare. Imagine dying of thirst, unable to take a drink … that agony would be minimal to what I believe an artist feels about losing the ability to become one with the canvas ever again. The injury would not heal unless the aggravation (the typing) stopped. After the surgery, I decided to leave my job in order to heal. Leaving was also about finally being true to myself. My soul was at risk of dying behind a desk, unable to express my personal creativity. With three months of savings, I quit my 9 to 5 job and decided to work on my art and photography. I took a chance on me. I left the safety of the harbor and dove deep into the ocean of my life, allowing the waves of healing to wash over me.

My soul grew full, and that's all that mattered. I joined a medical weight-loss program, but I realized that I still needed more. As I continued to work on myself, I found and attended a meeting on childhood trauma. I learned that women who are abused as children are at higher risk of developing heart disease and cancer in their reproductive organs. I was stunned; I realized that I had carried that trauma in my womb throughout my life, and that trauma took away the ability for me to have children. I had lost a significant piece of my womanhood. I joined the twelve-step recovery program at FA (Food Addicts in Recovery Anonymous) and learned about why I ate, when I ate, and how I used food as an attempt to fill what was *actually* empty inside of me. I discovered what my real hunger was.

I was ready to pursue my photography as a career and to really capture the true essence within people. I've always easily connected with people, and I wanted to use this gift to bring their soul-self out in their images. I started attending women's networking events and conferences. At one, I met a woman named Caterina who told me I was going to be a speaker. A speaker! Me?? A fat, unworthy, abandoned, and very self-conscious victim? I was never going to stand in the room and speak. But Caterina invited me to join one of her speaking workshops for free, and, soon after, I was invited to speak at a women's self-care event. With not much speaking experience, I vulnerably, courageously, and very fearfully told my story for forty-five minutes. When I was done, there was not a dry eye in the room. Several women came up to me and said, "I have the same story and have never been able to speak about it." I knew then that speaking would become one of the paths I would follow. And I have. Every time I tell my story, I don't just help others but heal a part of myself.

Relationships and Radical Awakening

In 2015, I met a man with whom I connected effortlessly. This angel of a human being and I had a very beautiful, soulful, energetic connection that was very pure. It was my first real and serious relationship, and I couldn't have picked a better person to experience it with. Ultimately, we got engaged. But I was still in the throes of the work I needed to do to heal myself, and he was living in the Netherlands. I couldn't expect him to uproot his life and walk a road not even I was familiar with. And I didn't believe I was truly ready for it. I was too needy and dependent, and I relied heavily on him. He was an incredible man who supported me through many struggles, including cancer. But my demons and my brokenness haunted the relationship.

I walked away from an engagement to a man I loved very much to work on myself. To this day, I am proud of my bravery and courage to trust myself and put my healing first. We remain friends. Ancient Greek has different names for love including *philia*, *eros*, and *agape*. Each defines a different kind of love, and each meets the needs of various spaces within us. Through the connection we shared, we were able to keep the flame of *philia*, the friendship love, alive even though the *eros*, the passionate love, flame had gone out. He revealed layers of my soul ... revealed parts of me that helped me to better understand my needs and allowed me to see that I had used external people, places, and things to complete myself, and why, despite my most desperate attempts, I remained incomplete.

On June 16, 2017, I met another beautiful soul who changed my life forever. The depth of his voice penetrated into my essence, and

I felt a familiar connection. As Rumi said, "Lovers don't accidentally meet somewhere, they exist in each other all along." We had a unique, unconventional long-distance relationship. He accepted and loved all parts of me in a way I had never experienced before. He taught me how to fall in love with my reflection. But I hadn't done any work to heal myself since my engagement had broken off, so I took my wounded self with me into this new relationship. Though I tried to enjoy it with no expectations, my heart, my soul, and every cell of my existence breathed his essence, and attachment was inevitable. Our union in person was nothing less than magical, mystical, and miraculous. I had been in love before and given my heart away, but I had never surrendered my soul to another. Every time our gazes met, I saw the divine in him.

But a future together was doomed because of cultural and societal reasons completely outside of our love, and we separated.

Kahlil Gibran said it best: "Love knows not its own depth until the hour of separation." Although it was the most heavenly love I had ever known, it was also the most painful, the most devastating, and left me shattered beyond recognition. It brought me to my knees. I had been heartbroken before, but this pain made me want to tear my skin off. For two years, I woke up on a drenched pillow and went to bed with silent sobs. Just breathing made me physically ache.

After merely existing for those two years, I began to understand that the pain was there to help my soul evolve. It was my awakening. I isolated myself and addressed every wound that was triggered. As I fearlessly stepped into my true spiritual being and awareness, I realized there's no such thing as separation in the world of our souls. He is me, and I am him—we're always connected!

From that point on, I kept him safely tucked away in the most sacred corner of my heart, and I continue to water that corner with a drop of unconditional love every day. That place of my heart is forever in bloom. When I was in the midst of despair, I never imagined the love that gave me the deepest agony would be the same love that would free, awaken, enlighten, and unite me with my pure divinity. As Rumi says, "The one that truly loves you will set you free." Love does not need to attain, possess, own, or even be in the presence of. Love just loves. It was a radical awakening.

I relied on my ex-fiancé during this time, and, with his support, I came to understand that I should not dwell on the past or worry about the future. I should live in the present. He also saw that I needed to do so on my own, that it was time for me to stand on my own two feet and to use everything I had learned to grow and move on. He believed I was ready and capable of facing my next chapter, the world, without him. While this initially triggered my abandonment issues, I was not the same person I had once been. I was going to go at it on my own.

My Story Guides My Work

By 2019, in the wake of the separation, I had given up on my business of helping others through photography and art. I wanted to get a job. I felt more comfortable letting someone else be responsible for my life because the fear of failing was a shadow that lurked in the corners and followed me everywhere I went.

I applied for a job at Delta Airlines and underwent a rigorous recruitment process. It took four months of intense interviewing and answering questions to land the job—to be selected from twenty thousand other applicants! I had been chosen; I was seen. I received the job of a lifetime, but it would be short lived. COVID-19 was on the horizon. When it hit, my job offer was rescinded. Nevertheless, the impact of the offer itself on my self-esteem and self-value was priceless. The seed that was faith in my abilities had been planted earlier, but this offer had helped it grow.

During the pandemic, I felt like a ship lost at sea, with no crew to rely on and no chart or map to set my course to. I withdrew into myself, gardening and grounding myself in the earth. While I gardened, I would listen to motivational videos. One day, I came across a video of Wayne Dyer. I listened to one video then another and another and kept listening everyday and throughout the day for months. When the student is ready, the teacher appears. He's the one teacher that completely transformed my life and fully connected me to my purpose.

Following are the three main lessons I learned and embodied from him.

1. There are no justified resentments. I went all the way back, took an inventory, and forgave anyone that I felt had ever caused me pain. I released my grudges which freed that energy from within me. At any given time, everyone is doing what they think is best according to their level of consciousness and life experiences. We either carry resentment and make it personal and suffer, or use it to empower us.

2. Our soul already knows what its purpose is. Therefore, it's going to orchestrate events in our lives that we need to transcend in order to fulfill our purpose. Even as a child I knew that my purpose was to help people that are suffering through pain. And so life gave me a myriad of painful experiences to overcome so that I would be able to help others heal. After all, I can't heal people if I've never experienced pain myself. Every thing that ever happened to me and all the people that came into my life that caused me pain were, in fact, tools to help me arrive at my purpose. Understanding this changed my whole perspective. I not only forgave, but I'm grateful for the experiences, and I have a lot of compassion for them all. Only

hurt people hurt people, and one's life has to be so small to take power from a four-year-old.

3. You can only give what you have inside. We are all born as pure love, but we become conditioned as life happens and, thus, learn fear. As our ego develops and wants to keep us safe, we detach from our pure unconditional love consciousness and begin to exist in a state of fear and suffering. To process this, I began to go deeper into myself and unlearn everything I thought I was. I shed all the layers that kept me supposedly protected, but, in reality, had acted as a barrier between me and my sovereignty. I decided to fully embody and become unconditional love. Now that is all I have to give and that's all I see in everyone else. I fearlessly stepped into my true essence and began following my heart's true calling and sharing the creative gifts I had been blessed with.

During the pandemic, I created a coaching program that uses an art meditation to connect us to our sovereign selves, to heal the inner child, to dissolve the trauma of molestation, and to help fully accept ourselves just as we are—mind, body, and soul. My soul-based programs help me utilize all the gifts I have been blessed with. As a painter, I no longer just paint on canvas. I feel, heal, unfold, express, and tell poetic stories of my soul's journey.

It all started with the willingness to heal myself and do the inner work. I was tired of the patterns repeating and being in a constant state of suffering. The root of it all is the inner child. Though I had begun to address the things that *she* had been through, I always saw her as separate from me. This was not really healing. But we were both desperate to heal and connect with one another. Because I was ready for this union with her, the universe sent me a gift in Marty Ocean Eagle. He was placed in my path to help me bridge the gap between me and my inner child. He was a random beautiful stranger that I met on Facebook who said to me, "I don't know how we are supposed to help each other, but there is something we need to do together." I agreed, and we met for coffee one evening. I felt so much love and safety from him. He kindly asked me if he could hold one of my hands and put his other hand on my heart, and I permitted it. His eyes welled up, and he said, "I don't usually see visions but I saw a little girl about four or five years old in a canoe in the middle of the ocean and she's lost and afraid and needs to come home. Can you bring her home?" At that moment I realized that *I* had to provide this child with everything she needed. I abandoned her—she was never abandoned by anyone else. And so I set forth on the journey to really unite with her—through writing, through meditation, through whatever means I could. My relationship and my understanding of her and her needs were gradually being elevated and fulfilled.

I started to see everything with love: molestation started my process to my soul's work; I was never abandoned; cancer blessed me; heartbreak united me with myself; not being accepted and body-shamed pushed me to shed the weight that didn't serve me; self-harm helped me to survive. Everything was always happening for me and not to me. This enabled me to learn to love more and give more to everyone. It was all a gift, bringing me back to love myself deeper each time, bringing me back to my pure divine sovereignty. I am no longer giving and trying to please from an empty cup but selflessly giving from my overflow because my cup is constantly filled from within. Today I am completely fulfilled and free at the same time. Having reached this place in my life, these are the lessons I share with my clients, and with you:

1. Embrace your pain with open arms and love your rock bottom with everything you have. It will take you to places beyond your imagination.

2. Surrender, then surrender beyond that, and when you think you can't surrender any more, surrender some more. For in surrender lies the infinite.

3. Everything you've ever wanted, needed, or sought for yourself, you already are. There's nothing you need to do or achieve to be sovereign. Right now each one of you is divinely whole.

Because I had the courage to heal myself, I have been able to create a beautiful and successful life. My internal world is the source of my external world. As a result of my healing, I can now share it with the world: the how and the why. And in a world where much pain exists, it is my intention to share my gifts of being a healer, a creator, and an empath through the effortless connection I am now able to cultivate with others. The pain was the path all along.

Today I use all my gifts to help people heal, come into their power, and learn to live their lives in authentic truth through my work as a certified transformational speaker, healer, artist, and coach. I am no longer the "fat, abandoned, unworthy victim." I am now an unconditionally loving, sovereign, empowered being here to light the path for others.

And it is truly a blessing to help others heal. Working together, I help my clients focus on their inner selves and heal what aches to transform their lives. They learn to develop resiliency and enhance their creativity. I guide them to recognize that their pain is their healing, their biggest gift, their savior, and their freedom from self. If they don't fully embrace their pain without resistance and allow it to move through them, the suffering will never end. I teach them to become courageous and use their struggles and the pain that they have produced to reach their goals, pursue their vision, and fulfill their purpose. And then, together, we transform their adversity into art. By centering them in art and photography in my coaching programs, I bring body and soul, flesh and spirit together so that they can share their stories and find healing and transformation. Afterall, we are pieces of art in motion.

Already through this work, I have collected the stories of many warriors, heroes, and magnificent beings that have overcome the most difficult challenges and transformed their pain into something inspiring for themselves and for all those that need hope. I have had the honor and privilege of capturing their stories by recreating their experiences with still images and painting them in their power. Together we've created a masterpiece of their struggles.

Surrender to the pain. May your life be a canvas. May you allow the beauty of your pain to reveal your majesty, divinity, and sovereignty and allow it to transform you into the masterpiece you are.

> *We are all stars wrapped in skin.*
> *The light you seek has always been within.*
> ~ Rumi

ABOUT NAFSHEEN LUHAR

Nafsheen Luhar has dedicated her life's work to radical self-love. As a survivor of cancer, self-harm, and molestation, she discovered that sharing her story and honoring her power through vulnerability allowed her to use her story to connect with others who have experienced trauma. Transforming the way she views herself through acknowledging and celebrating her pain, Nafsheen has mastered resiliency and broken free from her self-created prison. Using her gifts of creativity and the power of the soul's voice, Nafsheen teaches her clients to cultivate courage and change their pain into an opportunity to reach their highest purpose. Through a combination of Reiki, coaching, photography, and art, Nafsheen brings together body, soul, and spirit to help her clients tell their stories and turn their adversities into masterpieces of art.

Nafsheen is a highly-sought-after speaker and individual and group art and meditation leader. When she's not helping others heal, she can be found revealing the secrets of the universe through her camera lens, taking long road trips with her beautiful mother, or immersed in the pages of fascinating books. Nafsheen lives Rumi's words: "Our task is not to seek for love, but merely to seek and find all the barriers within ourselves that we have built against it."

To book a healing session with Nafsheen or to explore her creations, go to nafsheen.com.

The stories we tell literally make the world. If you want to change the world, you need to change your story.

— Michael Margolis

MY WISHES FOR YOU
Raul Lopez Jr.

You're reading this because you desire personal growth and understanding. And I'm writing this in hopes that my story of personal growth and understanding might inspire you on your journey.

Learn Your Life's Purpose

A frustrated person is one without a true sense of purpose. Yet, you were born to succeed and create something that no one else except you can accomplish. You are God's own idea, and He believes in you. So find and understand the "whys" in your life to get on the path of health and happiness.

How?

Consider the reasons—your heartfelt reasons—that are big enough for you to take action and achieve your goals. What do you want? Why do you want it? If the reasons you come up with aren't big enough, you will find excuses. And if you are noticing yourself making excuses, search again, deep within, until you find the reasons that stir your soul.

Once you find your reasons—your "whys"—you'll be at the start of your new path. Where to next? You might be stymied by this question. But the first right answer is to just step forward. In dozens of studies over the years, scientists have found that there is one major difference between successful people and unsuccessful people: successful people launch. They start. They get on with it. They just do it. Unsuccessful people get the same ideas and the same information, but they always have an excuse for not starting.

Have no fear. Stand and take charge of your destiny.

Your "whys" are clarity in your heart. The "hows" come next.

Your Mind Is Your Most Powerful Tool

First, learn to conquer your mind. With your "whys" understood, your mind will no longer be able to say no because your heart and mind are aligned!

But don't let your mind trick you into doubt. The human mind is powerful, and, thus, can also be destructive. It can be your greatest friend or your worst enemy. The person you see in the mirror will always provide your greatest challenges in life. Take control of your life by taking control of your mind. Understanding that you have the power to choose your thoughts is key. Being positive comes easy when everything is going your way. But when everything is going against you, that's when you must ask burning questions and seek answers.

Take charge of your thoughts for your thinking will lead to your actions. Making good decisions begins with how you view the world and others around you. Think loving thoughts about yourself as well as others.

Your mind is powerful. Make it work for you not against you.

Be in the Moment and Appreciate What Is Great in Your Life

Consider this: All that you need is within you now. You don't need material things to awaken from within. This moment is your key to a happy, successful life. Be aware of all the miracles around you and that are a part of you, right now. Appreciate everything in the moment. When you do, you make choices with more quality, connection, and love. Then, you can take control of your life at a given moment to pave that path to a better future.

Whatever comes your way in life, make the most of it. Choose to find a way to frame the experience as a valuable lesson or as giving you greater perspective. Decide to be grateful even for the difficult lessons for they make you a stronger and wiser person.

Afterall, the first step toward happiness is to be grateful. The truth is your life will start to change right now if you are grateful. Calm your mind. Get away from the noise of the world and think for a moment about what you can be grateful for like the air in your lungs or the life in your body. Become grateful that you have the opportunity to take your life to a whole new level.

At those inevitable times that you are upset, remind yourself that it is just in your mind. Tell yourself, "I'm more than these thoughts. I have a heart and soul. I love my life. I am powerful. I am free. What can I appreciate? What am I grateful for? How can I use this challenge to grow?"

When you are more connected with everything you do, there is greater success on all levels. Your journey through life becomes more joyful and effortless.

Create Your Own Heaven on Earth

It takes a conscious decision to choose and pay attention to the thoughts that make you feel good. Then, like anything else you practice, it becomes a habit, a new way of living. Allow yourself to feel good in as many moments as possible. The momentum will build.

If a situation is difficult for you, choose a better thought. Think of a specific moment that you felt joy. Close your eyes right now, and think of a wonderful event. Go back to that special moment and picture yourself there as if it were happening right now. Feel like you felt that day—joyful and happy. Breathe like you were breathing, smile and allow happiness in your life. You can do that anytime you want. Anytime you feel down, go back to that day, and immediately your mindset will change.

You were made to have a wonderful life. Don't let negative thinking make you miss out. Holding consistently negative thoughts and beliefs will bring you down. Take a moment to read that phrase again. When you change the way you look at things, the things you look at change.

So, decide to be the most positive person you know. Shift from making excuses about negative feelings to creating results. Start small. First, ask yourself, "What am I going to focus on?" Whatever you focus on is what you'll create and who you'll become. Up to this point, what have you focused on? Recognize how your focus has created your circumstances. Focusing is different than wanting. When you think about what you want, are you focused on the obstacles or the goal?

Your past has been full of lessons that have prepared you for your future. Make these lessons count by learning from them.

Dare to Dream

No circumstance, either good or bad, is insurmountable. There is always a solution; as Walt Disney said, "If you can dream it, you can do it." This means that you are never given a dream that you do not have the capacity to fulfill. You may have to learn some new skills, partner up with someone, and learn how to access new resources along the way, but all of that is possible if you'll simply dream the big dream.

Open your mind to everything and attach it to nothing. When you close your mind to what is possible, you close off the genius that lives within you.

See the Invisible, Do the Impossible

Anything you want *is* possible. Yes, it's true. Read that again: Anything you want *is* possible!

When you imagine your success before it even happens, you are on your way to achieving it. That's what the greats do, and *you are full of greatness.*

You are a perfect reflection of the choices you have made. If you want a better life, make better choices. Our universe is governed by the law of cause and effect or the law of attraction. Your intent and your actions directly create your experiences. A pure heart will find itself experiencing joy.

You have the power to create the life you want if you overcome your fear of failure. Don't let a fear of failure outweigh your desire to succeed. When you are willing to fail, when you decide you are unstoppable, when you make up your mind to become a no-matter-what person, you will then give birth to a part of yourself that can succeed.

Commit to Reaching Your Goals

Decide, commit, and resolve. Know that you deserve to experience how great life can be.

That is what takes you from the moment of change and carries you into the future even when things are difficult.

When writing the story of your life, make sure you hold the pen. Be brave and write the script from your heart. It's your story. There are no limits to what you can have, what you can do, or what you can be. You owe it to the world to be that positive change to inspire others who will say, "He did it. She did it. And I can do it, too."

Push Through the Discomfort

The comfort zone is your enemy. You are here to grow. Life will push you out of your comfort zone. One of the biggest ironies is living life trying to stay comfortable. Life will send more and more discomfort if you're too concerned about staying comfortable instead of growing and reaching a higher place.

So either commit to being on a journey of constant growth and feeling discomfort of your own accord, and become the master of your own destiny. Or hand over the keys, and let life happen to you instead. One path leads to success while the other leads you to constant struggle and pain.

Change Takes Discipline

Change is a campaign of discipline, hard work, and dedication.

Don't fall into the trap of trying to improve yourself with one magical change—one thing to change that will make your dreams come true. It isn't one thing or even ten things. Change doesn't come quickly; there are no shortcuts. It's a daily practice; sometimes even an hourly fight against weakness, temptation, or laziness.

Make important decisions with your heart, not your head. Your head will lead you down the wrong path because it only understands the logical world. Your heart and soul, however, speak truth. If you want to achieve results, then you have to become somebody different. You must upgrade your skills, choose better behaviors, and take charge of your emotions.

And, whatever you do, don't stop at failure. Everyone fails, but failure itself is a powerful tool to get back on the path.

Do Not Compare Yourself to Others

Develop a quiet inner confidence. This does not mean walking into a room with a cocky stride and telling yourself that you're better than everyone. It is the opposite. Try walking in knowing that you don't have to compare yourself to anyone. Comparing yourself to another person should not be part of who you are. A truly confident person has no thought of comparison. You are not above anyone; you are not below anyone. Get to the place in your life where you are good enough, not to others, but to yourself. That is confidence.

Lead the Pack

They say the wolf on the hill is never as hungry as the wolf climbing the hill. Be the wolf climbing the hill. Stay hungry. Never give up. Always look forward to the next feast. It is there waiting for you.

Set the standard for those around you. Don't let other people who are limited in their own accomplishments by their beliefs limit your beliefs. Block out fear and maintain a healthy mindset of your own. Rise up past your limitations and those of your family or friends.

Sometimes you must turn away from negative people in your life to move forward. You cannot be truly happy if you are always being the person others expect to see instead of the person you are meant to be.

Then, when you are truly yourself—your unique, fully-expressed self—great things start to happen. You'll attract the perfect people who will help you succeed. Success will come to you. Believe and achieve.

Believing in yourself—your abilities, resources, talents, and strength—is simply an attitude, and believing in yourself is a choice. You have to choose to believe that you can do anything that you set your mind to, because, in fact, you can.

Jumpstart your belief in yourself by speaking positive affirmations. They are powerful when practiced consistently. Say to yourself, "I can do all things. I love my life. I am powerful. I am strong. I am free." When you believe these positive statements, they send a message to your subconscious, which will then bring them into reality.

Giving to Others Is Life's Greatest Gift

If you want to create a better future for yourself, if you want to have a universal force backing you up, then from this point forward, it's essential that you purify your intentions and your actions, especially toward other people. You will never be happy if you are focused on making others miserable. You will never be successful if you wish others to fail. You will never live in prosperity.

So, let go of destructive thought patterns and behaviors. Choose your peers and distance yourself from toxic people who make it easier to make negative decisions. It may seem difficult at first to break away from or recognize the negative people in your life, but as you continue to learn, you will start to notice the people who bring you down.

Stop gossiping about your co-workers, about your neighbors, about the person driving too slow on the freeway. Leave all that behind. It hinders you. Find the beauty in yourself and in others. You will operate in kindness as a reflection of that beauty.

Motivational speaker Zig Ziglar said, "Help enough people get what they want, and the world will give you what you want."

When you make your life about giving—genuine giving—everything becomes far more meaningful. Ask, "How can I serve?" or "How can I improve the lives of all the people I encounter today?" It might simply be giving your time, some guidance, or an ear to listen.

Be Patient

Jim Rohn, a personal development speaker, said, "Stop focusing and expecting things to happen so fast. If you focus instead on building your skills, your gifts will make room for you."

Commit to mastery. If your goal isn't reached quickly, don't just start something new. Otherwise, you'll never know if you would have reached your goal because you didn't give it enough time to work.

You must set up a process that allows you to consistently grow. Once you have a clear goal, write it down. Make a written plan to achieve it, and then do at least one thing each day that moves you one step closer.

Decide right now that you are going to live your dreams, and never settle until you do.

ABOUT RAUL LOPEZ JR.

Raul Lopez Jr. is the creator of TAG Talks, and the author of *Heal the Boy and the Man Will Appear*. A leading self-development coach and motivational speaker, he is dedicated to teaching the importance of understanding and expressing emotions.

Raul has built two successful businesses and now teaches emotional intelligence in the form of e-motion (energy in motion). His personal development workshops teach how to eliminate fear, take action, and create the life you want.

To learn more about Raul and the work he does, visit raullopezjr.com.

Storytelling is the most powerful way to put ideas into the world today.

Robert McKee

THE BEST LAID PLANS
Jenny Infante-Reyes

"So, this is the plan ...."

I said this with conviction to my girlfriend as she came back with our Starbucks orders.

"First, I'm going to get promoted to marketing manager. And then ... and then Donny and I will get married. Then we'll buy the beach house with the balcony and the French doors ... and then when our careers ...."

She smirked and put the mocha latte to her lips. "Oh-kayyyyy ...." she responded back with a sliver of sarcasm. "Well, you *are* the planner!"

"Yes, I am the planner," I thought to myself, ignoring her tone. I sat back contently and sipped my hazelnut latte. "I could stick to the plan," I thought. It had been easy so far ....

- Graduate with honors. Check.

- Get into one of the country's top colleges in (what was recognized to be) *the* business program to take. Check!

- Land a brand manager role in one of the top multinational corporations. Check check!

Yes. Everything was going as planned.

Well ... not quite.

I didn't plan the sixty-hour work weeks that followed, month after month after month. I was always working, and my husband (then-fiancé) began to wonder if he'd really ever see me after our honeymoon. (Ultimately, there wasn't even a honeymoon because after we tied the knot on a Friday, I went back to work that Saturday. Hey, I had a marketing launch to pull off!)

I didn't plan to be misunderstood at every turn by my marketing manager and then told that not only was my next promotion questionable, but my position in the company was at risk. *What?!*

I didn't plan for everyday to be a struggle where I felt I constantly had to prove myself.

"Why do you still put up with it?" Kris, one of my best friends and a former colleague, had asked me one day when we were having our usual Starbucks waffle breakfasts and lattes.

Kris and I had met in a previous company and instantly bonded over coffee and marketing. She became a brand manager at another multinational, and we shared similar frustrations about the challenges in our positions and our companies.

"What do you suggest *we* do?" I asked. *We* being the operative word because I did *not* want to be alone in whatever it was that I felt was coming.

"We've talked about creating the solution to our brand management problems," she said. "So let's just do it!"

I stopped eating. "Meaning leave the safety net of our nice paying jobs for … uncertainty?!" Kris and I had often wondered what it would be like to leave corporate and dreamed about starting our own business. We just hadn't done it—yet.

"Well it's not *really* uncertain," Kris began to rationalize. "We know the problem. We work with agencies that can strategize but not implement and with implementing agencies with no strategy. We know we can do both. So let's go do it."

"And … we can work anywhere? We don't have to be in the office?"

"Yes! Cibo lunches forever," she said, and we laughed. Cibo was one of our all-time favorite restaurants.

Me? An entrepreneur? The thought was exciting. Scary. Promising.

It sounded like a plan.

Weeks later, I packaged up the last bits of my post-launch plan, turned in my resignation letter, and left the corporate world to co-create Your Brand Story.

With our shiny new Macbooks, lattes, and Cibo sandwiches, Kris and I built Your Brand Story to be the brand and marketing consulting firm that provided and integrated strategy and solutions that brought brands to life.

Fundamental to Your Brand Story is the belief that every business and every brand has a place in this world and is meant to solve a unique problem. It's a matter of finding what makes a brand stand out to the right audience. And what makes a brand stand out comes from a personal story. That's why we decided to call the company Your Brand Story.

A story is the foundation of any successful brand; it's what we based our own brand on. Afterall, your story sells! The original version of Your Brand Story's logo was an image of a book—because we were storytelling!

We approached other brand managers we knew and pitched our concept. Many loved it and bought into it; and because they knew the type of people we were and the work ethic we had, Kris and I soon had projects lined up for the rest of the year.

If I wasn't in a coffee shop or a restaurant, I worked from home. And while I did manage to see my husband more than he had anticipated, there was a part of the plan that hadn't yet fallen into place.

By the time we celebrated our second wedding anniversary, we still had not conceived a child.

Month after month and test after test, my OB/GYN threw at us everything she could think of. One exam here. Another of that vitamin there … have you thought of removing this food? What about if we checked this or that ….

Still—nothing.

"There's nothing wrong with you," my OB/GYN said after she looked over my chart one visit, as if she was reading my mind. "Maybe it's just not time."

"*Seriously?!*" I thought to myself. "Ugh. I give up. Maybe the kids aren't a part of the plan," I decided.

I distracted myself by throwing all of me into work. After all, Kris was expecting her first ("Hurray! A goddaughter for me!" I exclaimed when she shared the news), and business had to keep growing!

And grow it did!

We had a constant stream of clients and referrals. Your Brand Story grew to a team of seven employees plus trusted partners that were experts in their respective crafts. We made for a great team—very flexible, yet reliable. We were great at integrating strategy with execution.

The stress level was different. No one was putting pressure on me but me. It was on me—on us—to ensure that Your Brand Story's reputation stayed strong, relevant, and consistent. That was the focus.

And yet I still longed for a home and family life that seemed to have eluded me … and my plan.

"Not what I had planned."

I hit the button on the Keurig coffee maker in our little North Carolina apartment.

I debated opening the laptop to check on a brand concept that Kris sent over but couldn't bring myself to do it. I was so … very … tired.

It seemed like a different lifetime ago when Your Brand Story was building momentum in the Philippines and different parts of Asia.

But as we agreed to focus on our careers, my husband applied for further studies abroad. His acceptance letter came from North Carolina, and so we decided it was time to up and move.

I had a new plan: I thought about pursuing further studies of my own too.

But then as it turned out, I got pregnant.

My beautiful Sam came into our world after Thanksgiving that year (it was the turkey, I promise!), and ... two years and three months later, her sister Jamie followed.

And for three years, all I remember feeling was tired. "What was I thinking, wanting four kids? I'm completely overrun by two."

Growing up I was raised by a village—literally—for twenty-seven years. I had a nanny, aunts, uncles, and grandparents all available to help at a moment's notice. In North Carolina, it was me 24/7 all the time. No lifeline, no safety net. I was tired and I was torn. And I felt guilty. The time I spent on Your Brand Story dwindled.

I tried to keep up. With a pillow propped between my leg and my shoulder, I would hold a breastfeeding baby on the left and type an email with my right hand. Meanwhile, I would try to engage my little toddler with all the things she would bring to the table for playing together or allow her to watch another episode of *Elmo's World* while I worked.

When the girls were in bed at night, I would take Skype meetings in an opposite time zone.

I survived on very little sleep and a whole lot of coffee. But I tried.

I felt pressure to deliver and meet clients' demands, and I was worried that if I didn't bend over backwards, I would lose their business. I wasn't going to let that happen. I wanted to prove to myself I could, in fact, do it all.

Except I couldn't.

Your Brand Story took a backseat for the next few years as I learned every Kindermusik song, volunteered at every field trip, and attended every playdate. Don't get me wrong: I thoroughly enjoyed being there for all the milestones, but sometimes I felt a sadness that I couldn't explain.

A part of me longed for the discussions on advertising copy and launch plans. I missed the intellectual conversations on strategy and market share and business growth. I wished I had someone to brainstorm ideas with over lunch.

And then I felt guilty.

Here were the kids I had always wanted. But why did it still feel incomplete? And why did it always feel like an impossible choice?

If I was to be the loving, attentive, present mother, then could I not be the successful, independent, skilled entrepreneur too?

Everything just felt—messy. Disorganized. So out of order. And none of it—NONE—had gone according to my grand plan! Gaaaah!

"No thank you. I have other plans."

I surprised myself when I uttered these words.

She was a prospect referred to me by a former client. She had heard about Your Brand Story and was pleasantly surprised to know that it was now a limited liability company located in California—our new home.

Kris had moved on to be an independent consultant, and now that Sam and Jamie were in sixth and third grade, respectively, my husband hinted about becoming a double-income family once again.

Somehow I found small business owners in the area that needed basic branding help. So I would drop the girls at school and then pay these people a visit for a quick brand consultation. I might have spent everything I earned on gas and groceries, but hey … it was professional work.

I still wished, though, that something would change. I just wasn't sure how. It turns out, I didn't have to think very hard because the world took care of that.

When COVID shut the schools down and everything went online, suddenly everyone had a need for a remote brand consultant.

We turned our guest bedroom into the Your Brand Story office, and I began to take calls. I accepted everything that was coming my way. Some clients would ask for a heavy discount. "Why not?" I reasoned. "It was still money in the bank." It didn't matter what they paid me, I worked the same amount of time regardless.

It just so happened that this particular call came on the day that the cake Jamie baked wasn't rising, and she melted down in tears. It caught me off guard. Normally something that trivial wouldn't have set her off.

And then I found out that Sam was quite the ball of emotions too. "What's the point? I don't see my friends. I can't go out. I missed my promotion … why would I even bother to do anything?" said my tween, her voice breaking.

THE BEST LAID PLANS

The lockdown was taking its toll on my girls.

All of this had been brewing in my home for weeks, and because I was so busy rebuilding my dream business, I almost missed the signs. My heart broke.

We needed to get out of the house.

"But I needed you yesterday," said the prospect when I negotiated for a different day. "I'll pay you fairly."

For a brief moment I thought about the opportunity I was giving up. Then I remembered a training I had recently done about finding my deepest why. Why was I creating this dream business in the first place?

It was for them—Sam, Jamie, Donny—and for me. It was for a life where we could be happy and connected and free. So what was the point of throwing myself into building something if things were falling apart at home?

The choice was clear.

I politely declined the opportunity, put the phone down, and loaded up the car for the beach. The girls were bewildered, but went along with it anyway … seeing as how everyone just needed some escape.

On the beach with my coffee tumbler in hand, I let out one long breath as the girls ran into the waves. I pulled out the beach chair and watched as they built sand tunnels and mermaid tails. The waves crashed over their creations, and they squealed in delight.

A sense of calm washed over me. For the first time in a long time, it clicked. There was no guilt. No feeling of an impossible choice. No sadness for a missed opportunity.

I was where I was supposed to be.

This is how it's going to be done from now on. This is the new plan.

In the months that followed, things began to shift. I wrote down what I wanted Your Brand Story to become. I wanted to be a partner in building meaningful brands and not just someone that was hired to do a job. "No more one and done," I said.

I got clear on what was acceptable and what wasn't. Meetings on weekends were out. Those were the days with my girls when we'd stay in bed or make pancakes in the morning and just be together.

Also out were the heavy discounts and long negotiations. I finally began to trust the value I brought to the table. And if someone didn't see it that way, then maybe it wasn't our time to work together.

Time went by very quickly, and I soon had clients who valued my work ethic and trusted in my gifts, my knowledge, and my skills. They trusted me to carry out the work, to do it well, and to bring their brand to life. There was a mutual agreement and respect for each other, so much so that they were happy to work around my girls' piano recitals, as I would do the same for them.

I also let go of the clients that did not align with what I wanted. None of it came easy at first. It was nerve-wracking to say no to someone who was willing to pay good money. But if they didn't align with my values or respect some of my non-negotiables, then the money wasn't worth it.

"This is the new plan," I reminded myself each time I felt nervous. I had to trust it would all work out.

"Thank you.
This is better than I could have ever planned."

I was text-chatting with a client. We'd been collaborating on her business for about two years. It was really hard to see her as *just* a client. She had become more—a dear friend, a confidante, a colleague, someone I knew I would love to do life with for a long, long time.

We had exchanged several messages about some pending items for her business, mixed in with silly GIFs for fun and stories about our kids and our lives in general.

"I have to get the girls from school, but I sent you the latest invoice based on our agreement," I wrote.

She texted back: "Yes I saw it. I sent it back because … I believe we should double it."

My jaw dropped in surprise and gratitude. This had never happened to me before! I thanked her immensely.

"You're welcome! I truly appreciate you and all you do for me and my business," she continued. "And I'd love to chat about your idea tomorrow—after piano?"

I laughed out loud. She knew my family's schedule.

I agreed. "Of course. Thanks again!" I sent one final GIF that garnered me a laughing emoji.

I headed out the home office and down the stairs to grab my cup of coffee. Hazelnut Nespresso was today's pick as I hit the button that said "brew."

- Meetings done for the day. Check!

- Renewal contracts sent. Check!

- Girl Scout cookies delivered. Check!

Now it was time to get the girls and drive them to their activities. I sent a message to my husband and asked him to pick up dinner.

"Netflix date night later?" I asked.

"Sure, if you don't fall asleep again," he joked with a wink emoji. I laughed because it was true. Girl talk with my girls in bed and a cozy blanket was the perfect recipe to get me to sleep. Winter, our Maltipoo, jumped up from her cushion and ran to block the door with her thirteen-pound body, as if to say, "Take me with you!" I smiled.

Looking at Winter, the puppy that I said I would never have, reminds me daily of how different my life is from any plans I had made.

I have clients that I love that have renewed their engagements with me. And the best part is, they have become lifelong friends.

I've built a network of strategic partners that support my work and collaborate with me to bring brands to life. We trust each other, and we come together to support one another.

I attend recitals, I volunteer at school, I have boba time with Jamie, and pizza dates with Sam.

I have coffee dates with my husband. It is, as he jokes, the best way to keep me awake.

I'm there for it all—the fun, the laughter, the frustration, and the tears.

It's still sometimes messy and disorganized, and often out of order. In fact, the daily juggle is real. But it no longer is a struggle.

And I figured out that missing piece. It was me.

Me being me—all of me—all the time.

I get to live this life. This isn't at all a life that I had imagined—or could have ever planned.

It's better.

I wouldn't trade it for anything in the world.

ABOUT JENNY INFANTE-REYES

Jenny Infante-Reyes is a strategic brand integrator and marketing consultant. Her business, Your Brand Story, is designed to guide and support visionaries, business owners, and entrepreneurs in creating and growing their million-dollar businesses and bringing their brands to life.

Jenny has consulted on many businesses in all parts of the world across multiple industries. Her background and experience in both corporate and entrepreneurial marketing allows her to help big businesses, small businesses, and entrepreneurs and offer various brand and marketing solutions that cater to their needs.

Outside of her Kellogg Executive Education in Strategic Marketing, Communications, and Leadership, Jenny is also a certified Human Behavior Consultant. This is a core part of her practice as she believes that true and lasting growth deeply relies on one's awareness of self and others and how that is communicated and translated into personal and professional relationships. Additionally, Jenny is a #1 international best-selling author.

Jenny currently resides in California with her husband, her two girls, and their Maltipoo named Winter.

To connect with Jenny and learn more about Your Brand Story, visit yourbrandstory.co.

Great stories happen to those who can tell them.

— Ira Glass

YOUR STORY IS YOUR SUPERPOWER
Ellie D. Shefi

The Impact of Your Story

Have you ever looked around and thought to yourself, "How did I get here?"

Like you've been living your life as a character in someone else's story? A life driven by someone else's dreams, desires, demands, labels, and expectations? A life dictated by your past, your circumstances, or the stories you tell yourself about it all?

I get it. I've been that secondary character, living a life where I so badly wanted to be seen, heard, valued, and loved for myself. A life where I desperately wanted things to be different, but felt hopelessly lost, alone, and powerless to make them so. A life where I needed someone to guide me along my path of healing and growth—someone to share their story and their wisdom—someone to light the way.

Bit by bit, story by story, I became inspired and empowered. And bit by bit, story by story, I progressed. Through almost five decades of getting back up every time life has knocked me down, I've developed tools to break free from external expectations, create an impervious mind, and live life on my terms.

In the process of rewriting my life's story, I've learned what makes me unique—what makes my combination of knowledge, skills, experience, and passion distinct from anyone else's. What only I can offer the world. How my transparency and authenticity can serve the world while generating income. I've harnessed the power of my individual story and its unique impact. And now I get to embrace the magic that comes with sharing my story with others.

When you tell your story, you're owning your journey and proclaiming to yourself and others that no matter who you are or what you've experienced, *your message matters*!

You see, while it's true that I'm an attorney, advisor, #1 international best-selling and award-winning author, publisher, keynote speaker, strategist, consultant, corporate trainer, media host, and coach, it's also true that I'm an abuse survivor, a rape survivor, and a former anorexic who still struggles with body dysmorphia. I've struggled financially, lived in my car, and eaten the food restaurants were throwing away at the end of the night. I'm a cancer survivor and a medical miracle. For over two decades, I've defied the doctors' death deadlines. I've had thirteen major surgeries, and underneath my clothes, my body is covered in scars.

I have crawled, clawed, and scratched my way through fire after fire, and through it all, I have emerged a limitless thriver, problem solver, and opportunity creator, who chooses to live life with unending optimism. I have mastered turning fear into faith and pain into purpose. It's my life's mission to use my voice, to share my message with the world, and to empower others to do the same.

As hard as my story has been to live at times, I know that someone in the world is waiting to hear it—to be inspired by it, to be empowered by it, and to know that they are not alone. I am transparent about my darkest moments and the strength they've begotten because my story will resonate with and attract those who need to hear it. Someone in the world is waiting for me to shine my light and help guide them on their path. When I tell my story—when I reveal my scars—I can impact lives and change the world!

Scars Reveal Authentic Stories

We delight in the beauty of the butterfly, but rarely admit the changes it has gone through to achieve that beauty.
~ Maya Angelou

Scars. We all have them. Some are visible. Others are not. Some we are conscious of. Others lurk in the shadows. Some are from childhood. Others have grown over the wounds adulthood and independence bring. Some are physical. Others are mental and emotional. Regardless of their type or origin, everyone has them. I have them. You have them. Your best friend has them. The person standing behind you in the line at the grocery store has them. The server who brings you your meal at a restaurant has them. The biggest stars in the world have them. We *all* have them.

Though our scars have shaped our histories and our life paths, they do *not* define us. Scars are stories of survival, of strength, of growth. Your scars are reminders that you are stronger than you ever thought possible—that you have persevered and overcome every obstacle that life has put before you. Your scars are reminders that you are a relentless force. Your scars form the basis of the chapters of your life story!

And, like scars, which are literally layer upon layer of healing strength, you, too, are the embodiment of resilience. You *can* intentionally and deliberately write a new chapter for your life—a life that YOU define; that YOU create—a life where YOU decide *your* dreams, *your* desires, *your* passions, *your* values, and *your* vision for a life of impact, meaning, and purpose! Leverage that healing strength to empower yourself and share your experience with the world. Not only will you be the embodiment of resilience, you'll become an example of it to others.

When you accept and even embrace your scars, you create space to define for yourself who you are, what you stand for, and what you want out of life. You can write the empowering story of *you*. And you'll find that your story becomes the gateway to the life and impact you desire. Instead of being ashamed of your scars, be transparent about them—the stories behind your scars are the stories of your authentic self. They are the stories that others are waiting to hear, that build trust, that resonate with your ideal clients, and that enable them to relate to you and choose you!

Change Your Story, Change Your Life— Share Your Story, Change the World

Step out of the history that is holding you back.
Step into the new story you are willing to create.
~ Oprah Winfrey

Words, and the meanings you assign them, are incredibly powerful. In fact, the words you attach to your experiences actually *become* your experiences! Have you ever noticed that the more you tell people you're tired, the more tired you feel? The more you tell people you're stressed, the more stressed and overwhelmed you feel? The more you tell people a story about how someone betrayed you, the more betrayed and angry you feel? The words you use and the stories you create about a situation are more powerful than the situation itself! Your words, your thoughts, and your stories either empower you or imprison you. What stories are you telling yourself about things that have happened to you?

I know you can't choose what's happened to you. Believe me, I do. But what I also know is that when you change the story you tell yourself about what's happened to you, you change your life.

I'm not telling you to ignore the events of your life. They happened. No one can wave a magic wand and erase them from your life. What I *am* saying, though, is that when you change the words you use to describe your thoughts, feelings, and life events to reflect an empowering narrative, you take control and write your own story. And with that story, you'll grow.

You may be thinking, "That sounds great, but how does this work in real life?" Let me show you:

My friend is a blind woman who was born to a poor family in rural India. In her village, it was common for daughters to be sold into marriage for a dowry. Being born blind, her mother and father knew that she would not attract a high dowry and they could not afford to feed her. Without a proper dowry, feeding her meant that someone else would starve.

One day, her mother took her by the hand and led her to a bus stop and left her there. Abandoned. Frightened. Alone.

For years, this was my friend's reality. This was her life story, and she lived with all of the painful feelings that story brought up. She often told herself the story of how her parents were embarrassed by her, how she brought shame to her family, and how she was such a burden they had to cast her aside in order to be free from the shame and financial burden that this poor, disfigured, blind girl imposed upon them. She told herself the story that she was worth so little that she could easily be discarded. She told herself the story that she was unlovable and unworthy. All of these feelings created an overflowing well of anger, pain, and resentment within her.

This story defined her, until one day she made a powerful decision. She decided that this was not the story of her childhood. She decided to change her story and change her life. She shifted her perspective and took control of her narrative.

Today, if you ask her what her life story is, she will tell you that she was born to a loving mother and father in a poor village in rural India. She will tell you that, being blind, her parents knew that even if they were able to find a husband who would be willing to pay a dowry for her, she might not be treated well. They worried for her future. The only way they could help her have a better life was to let her go.

So one day her mother summoned all of the courage within her so that she could do what she felt was the right thing for her beloved child. She took her daughter by the hand and led her to a well-lit bus stop near the police station, where she was sure to be found by a kind policeman. Not wanting to frighten her child or draw attention to what was happening right away, she sat her beloved daughter on the bench and quietly walked away. With tears in her eyes, she didn't look back.

As her mother had hoped, a kind policeman found her and took her to the safety of an orphanage, where she was adopted by an incredible family in Canada. She has been more loved by her adopted family than she ever thought possible. She is thriving every single day—all because her loving mother selflessly released her to a better life. Her mother loved her enough to let her go, and for that she is eternally grateful.

My friend's story is a powerful example. Although the events of her life are what they are—her mother left her as a very young blind girl at a bus stop near a police station in rural India—her story reminds us of the power of the words we use and the meanings we give them. As my friend so poignantly demonstrates, you can use the story you tell yourself about events in your life to either keep yourself in an emotional prison, or you can take the key and set yourself free. Changing the meaning she attached to the events of her past set her free. *For the first time in her life*, she allowed herself to feel loved, worthy, enough, wanted, and valued. Reframing her story allowed her to replace anger and resentment with empathy, compassion, and gratitude. Her shift in meaning didn't change the facts of what happened, but by changing her story, she found a new life and a new future. She found her message—her superpower! She came to understand that her message mattered, and she could have a profound and empowering impact by sharing her story.

You Are Your Source

You are the designer of your destiny; you are the author of your story.
~ Lisa Nichols

My friend came into my life and shared her story with me at a time when I needed a guide, an inspiration. After she came to deeply understand the power of her story and how it made her unique, and she came to realize that she had an important message that only she could share with the world, she was ready for it to make an impact. And I was there to receive it.

Soon after, it became my turn—my turn to rewrite my story, to find my unique message in preparation to share it with the world and amplify my impact. Rewriting my story involved breaking free from the chains of labels, expectations, and external demands—defining for myself who I wanted to be, what I wanted to stand for, and what I wanted my life to be. I GOT TO CHOOSE. I realized that *I am my source*. And I learned that my story is powerful in its authenticity.

I've picked myself up in moments when I didn't think I could, and I've decided time and time again to change my story, shift my perspective, and take control of my life. Since the moment I made that first powerful decision, with each subsequent twist and turn, I've consciously chosen empowering meanings and perspectives, and I've intentionally placed myself in the driver's seat, grabbed hold of that steering wheel, and hit the gas pedal toward destinations I set.

But it hasn't always been that way.

What was my turning point, you ask? I'm a domestic violence survivor. Things got bad. So bad that my health deteriorated and my life literally depended on the help of others to get me out. My removal from the situation took four police officers and my dad driving the getaway car. Two officers pulled me out of my apartment, two officers held my ex-husband back, and my dad stepped hard on the gas the second the officers put me in his car.

I was put into hiding and, for a while, I became a ghost. I was placed in a home with a man I didn't know. I was terrified. I barely left my room and had lost all ability to make a decision. Every single day for the rest of the year, I ate the exact same thing for breakfast, lunch, and dinner because no one told me what to eat, and I simply was not capable of making my own decisions or functioning independently.

Then, one day, after months of intense trauma therapy, something shifted in me. I finally understood that, if things were going to get better, I had to make a choice. I had to be the one to decide that my life was worth more, that I was worth more. I began changing my story. Instead of seeing myself as the girl whose future had been snatched from her, I decided to see my situation as an opportunity.

"I am complete ashes," I told myself. "This is ground zero for my life. What an incredible opportunity I have to start over from scratch and rebuild myself into exactly who I want to be. What an amazing gift that, in starting over, I get to define for myself who I will be, what

I will stand for, and how I will live my life from this point forward. What freedom!"

I recognized right then and there that my experiences were a blessing. I finally understood that I was powerful beyond measure, and that I actually had control over my life in all aspects—even those that I had thus far felt powerless to control. I realized that I had the power to write my own story, the way *I* wanted it to be ... not my parents, not my past, not society, and not labels placed on me by an outside observer. *Me.* I had the power! I became my own source of strength, light, and inspiration. I chose an empowering perspective and wrote the story I wanted to tell—the story that was a genuine reflection of who I determined I was going to be. I became the author of the unique story that is me!

And once armed with that story—that knowledge and experience that makes me unique—I've found others waiting to hear it ... waiting to be inspired ... waiting to feel my impact. Transparency, authenticity, and growth are woven throughout my story. And it is my story that allows people to trust me, believe in me, and choose me for guidance. It is my *story* that sells!

ABOUT ELLIE D. SHEFI

Ellie Shefi is an attorney, advisor, leadership consultant, corporate trainer, keynote speaker, strategist, and #1 international best-selling and award-winning author who helps organizations optimize their culture and individuals expand their influence.

As the founder of MTC Consulting, Ellie leverages her more than thirty years of experience in law, business, education, and advocacy to help organizations build resilient teams and world-class cultures while developing influential leaders. Serving as a strategic advisor to governments, universities, corporations, entrepreneurs, and NGOs, she has successfully helped organizations mitigate their risk, optimize their operations, and align their teams.

Through her signature programs: Monetize Your Expertise™, Monetize Your Message™, and Master the Media™, Ellie helps entrepreneurs, leaders, coaches, and consultants become global brands by sharing their story in books, on stage, and in the media.

Dedicated to empowering others to use their voice, Ellie founded Made to Change the World™ Publishing, a full-service independent publishing house, where she guides aspiring best-selling authors through the writing and publishing process and helps leaders amplify their message so they can scale their impact.

A sought-after speaker, Ellie is regularly interviewed in top publications and on podcasts and media channels like *Forbes*, *Entrepreneur*, NBC, ABC, and CBS, amongst others, and she hosts the *Free by Design*™ television show, the *Creating an Impervious Mind*® YouTube series, and the *You Are Not Your Scars*® podcast.

Ellie is also the founder of the Made 2 Change the World™ Foundation, an emerging nonprofit organization that equips and empowers the next generation with the tools, resources, and strategies they need to create the lives, communities, and world they envision.

To connect with Ellie and learn more about her services, visit ellieshefi.com.

A NOTE FROM ME TO YOU

You have read the stories of these remarkable men and women who have shared their knowledge, wisdom, and advice with you. It is my sincere hope that you found each of them as inspiring as I do! Reach out to them. Connect with them. Learn from them as you prepare to craft and share your own story. And should you stumble or ever feel confused or frustrated, just know:

You have greatness within you.
You are more powerful than you can ever begin to imagine.
You are greater than your circumstances; you don't have to go through life being a victim.

I applaud you for dreaming and for running toward your dream. I applaud you for believing in yourself because that's what life is about: stretching and challenging yourself, looking for ways that you can improve your life and the lives of others.

I applaud you for the vulnerability and sincerity it takes to embrace and share your story of your struggles and your growth, with transparency and authenticity. I applaud you for having the courage to share your story for prosperity and to heal and transform yourself and the world.

I applaud you for being you.

                        Yours in greatness,
                  Les Brown—Mamie's Baby Boy

YOUR MESSAGE MATTERS, YOUR STORY SELLS!

As you've undoubtedly come to realize as you've read the stories in this book, your voice matters. Your knowledge matters. *Your message matters.*

You were made to change the world. And it's through the *power of your story* that you'll create the impact you desire!

The contributors in this book have shared their powerful stories and revealed how their stories have enabled them to grow their businesses and become globally recognized brands. With their stories as their superpower, they have become undeniable experts in their fields and are impacting people around the world every day. Their story sells!

And so can yours! Your story is powerful! Shared with transparency and authenticity, your story will emphasize your growth and lay the foundation of your credibility. Your story makes you unique, and that uniqueness is the very thing that will drive your ideal clients to you. Your story is the gateway to the life and impact that you want.

Your story sells!

It's your turn now. Know the power of your story. Harness that power. Share your story! We can't wait to hear you change the world!

—Made to Change the World™ Publishing Team

REPRINTED WITH PERMISSION

Maya Comerota
Ellie D. Shefi
Les Brown
Jerremy Alexander Newsome
Kate Butler
Winnona Gaviglio
David Grace
Nafsheen Luhar
Raul Lopez Jr.
Jenny Infante-Reyes

*Each author in this volume of *Your Story Sells* holds the copyright to his or her individual contribution(s), and they have graciously given their permission for their stories to be shared herein.*

www.ingramcontent.com/pod-product-compliance
Lightning Source LLC
Chambersburg PA
CBHW050727010526
44107CB00009B/762